M000239991

REAL ESTATE LICENSE EXAM
Calculation Workbook

Coventry House Publishing

CONTENTS

INTRODUCTION

Dear Soon-to-be Agent,

Congratulations on your decision to embark in a career in real estate. It's with great pride that I consider real estate to be the best decision that I've ever made. Due to its nature as a competitive industry, I can also say that it's been one of the hardest things that I've ever done. But don't let that deter you. Any agent who has what it takes to be a top producer should expect a bit of difficulty along the way.

Learning the material in this guide is important for your future success because it will set the foundation for what is going to be an important aspect of working with clients and making sure that you are up-to-speed on guiding client decisions with great discernment and attention to detail.

In this book, you'll be tasked with answering a series of questions that will help you pass your real estate license exam. The materials also serve as a tool to help you brush up on knowledge that will help you effectively service your clients for years to come.

Becoming a real estate agent is an important life choice. We need qualified agents who are passionate about helping people, and who are passionate about learning as much as possible to know their market. But being dedicated is only part of the equation, you will also need knowledge. I'm on your side and have created products and services, such as this one, to help you become the best agent in your local market. Fortune is on your side!

Sincerely,

josh flagg

SECTION 1

LAND DESCRIPTION AND DEVELOPMENT

QUESTIONS

1. Alpha Real Estate Company owns a 35-acre tract of land. In order to develop it, they must set aside 5% of the area for a pond, and 15% for streets and sidewalks. If the minimum permissible lot size is 11,200 square feet, the maximum number of lots that can be developed is:

   A. 100.
   B. 104.
   C. 108.
   D. 112.

2. Diane purchased five rectangular lots containing a total of 44,000 square feet. If each lot is 110 feet deep, then each of her lots has _____ of road frontage.

   A. 80 feet
   B. 120 feet
   C. 160 feet
   D. 240 feet

3. If a lot represents 19% of a square mile, the lot size is:

   A. 115.9 acres.
   B. 118.4 acres.
   C. 121.6 acres.
   D. 124.5 acres.

4. David's lot sold for $330 a front foot. If the lot was 820 feet deep and had an area of 150,400 square feet, the selling price of David's lot was:

   A. $60,526.82.
   B. $62,412.06.
   C. $64,601.34.
   D. $66,295.70.

5. The number of square feet in 3 acres is:

   A. 126,390.
   B. 128,580.
   C. 130,680.
   D. 132,940.

6. Liz sold her 8.3-acre lot for $1,785,000. The price per square foot was:

   A. $4.90.
   B. $4.94.
   C. $4.97.
   D. $5.03.

7. A parcel of land is square, measuring ¾ mile by ¾ mile. The number of acres in the parcel of land is:

A. 320.
B. 360.
C. 480.
D. 560.

8. William recently purchased a lot measuring 130 feet by 175 feet. If he paid $201,500 for the lot, the price per front foot was:

A. $1,151.
B. $1,303.
C. $1,450.
D. $1,550.

9. Lori purchased a rectangular tract of land measuring 2,250 feet by 2,925 feet. The number of acres in the tract of land is:

A. 151.08.
B. 153.27.
C. 155.89.
D. 157.13.

10. Beta Corporation purchased a 12.2-acre tract of land. If 15% of the land must be used for drainage and other uses, the maximum number of 6,500 square foot lots that can be platted is:

A. 60.
B. 63.
C. 66.
D. 69.

11. The number of square feet in a section is:

A. 3,484,800.
B. 6,969,600.
C. 13,939,200.
D. 27,878,400.

12. Robert purchased a rectangular tract of land that contains 22.5 acres. If the measurement on one side is 865 feet, the depth of the land is:

A. 925 feet.
B. 1,133 feet.
C. 1,478 feet.
D. 1,690 feet.

13. Kyle is selling a tract of land measuring 1,150 feet by 2,050 feet for $950,000. The price per acre is:

    A. $17,533.33.
    B. $20,378.55.
    C. $23,602.57.
    D. $26,142.90.

14. Delta Holding Company would like to develop a subdivision containing 425 lots averaging 15,000 square feet. If an average of 1,750 square feet of street, sidewalks, and drainage must be provided for each lot, the number of acres the company will need to purchase to achieve their goal is:

    A. 155.76 acres.
    B. 158.98 acres.
    C. 163.42 acres.
    D. 168.34 acres.

15. The number of square miles in a quadrangle is:

    A. 288.
    B. 432.
    C. 576.
    D. 1,152.

16. April owns a 15-acre plot of land that she would like to develop into lots measuring 225 feet by 300 feet. The maximum number of lots that she can develop is:

    A. 7.
    B. 9.
    C. 11.
    D. 13.

17. Steven, a real estate developer, owns a 78.5-acre lot. The lot represents _____ of a square mile.

    A. 9.26%
    B. 10.44%
    C. 11.85%
    D. 12.27%

18. If land has a perimeter of 12 miles on each side, the number of townships is:

    A. 2.
    B. 3.
    C. 4.
    D. 5.

19. Caroline purchased a 2-acre lot for $6.15 per square foot and built a house measuring 85 feet by 85 feet. If the price of the house was $110.50 per square foot, Caroline's total cost was:

A. $1,321,912.70.
B. $1,326,487.40.
C. $1,331,095.20.
D. $1,334,150.50.

20. The number of acres in 2.5 square miles is:

A. 920.
B. 1,150.
C. 1,280.
D. 1,600.

21. Melissa purchased a 3,450-square foot house on 1.85 acres of land. The price was $140.50 per square foot for the house plus $38,250 per acre. The total price that Melissa paid was:

A. $549,572.25.
B. $555,487.50.
C. $558,385.90.
D. $563,975.85.

The following information relates to questions 22 – 25.
Derrick, a real estate developer, purchased a 32-acre tract of land. 25% of the land must be used for sidewalks and drainage, and zoning laws allow 3 lots per acre. Comparable lots are selling for $35,500, and 32% of the sale price of each lot must be allocated towards overhead and selling costs.

22. Based on the information provided, the number of lots that Derrick can develop is:

A. 24.
B. 72.
C. 96.
D. 128.

23. Based on the information provided, if all lots are sold, the gross sales price will be:

A. $852,000.
B. $1,704,000.
C. $2,556,000.
D. $3,408,000.

24. Based on the information provided, if all lots are sold, Derrick's total overhead and selling costs will be:

    A. $817,920.
    B. $1,363,200.
    C. $1,738,080.
    D. $2,556,000.

25. Based on the information provided, if all lots are sold, Derrick's profit will be:

    A. $817,920.
    B. $1,363,200.
    C. $1,738,080.
    D. $2,556,000.

26. The number of acres in a township is:

    A. 36.
    B. 1,296.
    C. 21,600.
    D. 23,040.

27. Geraldine purchased a property that measures ½ mile by ½ mile. The area of the property is:

    A. 3,484,800 square feet.
    B. 6,969,600 square feet.
    C. 13,939,200 square feet.
    D. 27,878,400 square feet.

28. The area of three sections is:

    A. 1,280 acres.
    B. 1,920 acres.
    C. 2,560 acres.
    D. 3,200 acres.

29. Charles is selling the NW ½, SW ¼, S ¼, W ¼ of a section. This is equivalent to:

    A. 217,800 square feet.
    B. 272,250 square feet.
    C. 340,313 square feet.
    D. 425,390 square feet.

30. According to the Public Land Survey System, a township has _____ sections.

    A. 8
    B. 16
    C. 24
    D. 36

The following information relates to questions 31 – 32.
Sigma Corporation is subdividing an 18-acre tract of land into lots measuring 90 feet by 125 feet. They have allowed 232,830 square feet for streets and common areas.

31. Based on the information provided, the total number of lots that Sigma Corporation can develop is:

    A. 45.
    B. 47.
    C. 49.
    D. 51.

32. Based on the information provided, if Sigma Corporation plans to generate gross income of $1,715,000, they will need to sell each lot for:

    A. $32,000.
    B. $33,000.
    C. $34,000.
    D. $35,000.

33. Jack purchased a lot measuring one-third of a mile by one-sixth of a mile. The area of Jack's property is:

    A. 34.28 acres.
    B. 35.56 acres.
    C. 36.72 acres.
    D. 37.96 acres.

34. Samantha, a real estate developer, needs to earn $1,033,500 from the sale of lots in a subdivision to recoup her investment. The subdivision contains a total of 64 acres, and 16.5% of the land is to be used for roads. If each lot measures 1 acre, and no partial lots are permitted, Samantha must charge _____ per lot to generate the desired income.

    A. $19,500
    B. $20,000
    C. $20,500
    D. $21,000

35. Marie purchased 5 adjacent lots, each measuring 75 feet wide by 165 feet deep. If the total cost of the lots was $142,900, the price per square foot was:

A. $2.18.
B. $2.23.
C. $2.27.
D. $2.31.

ANSWER KEY

1. C
Conversion factor: 1 acre = 43,560 sq. ft.
Step 1: Area for pond = 35 acres × 0.05 = 1.75 acres
Step 2: Area for streets and sidewalks = 35 acres × 0.15 = 5.25 acres
Step 3: Remaining area for lots = 35 acres – 1.75 acres – 5.25 acres = 28 acres
Step 4: Square feet for lots = 28 acres × 43,560 sq. ft. per acre = 1,219,680 sq. ft.
Step 5: Number of lots = 1,219,680 sq. ft. ÷ 11,200 sq. ft. per lot = 108.9 = 108 full lots

2. A
If each lot is rectangular and has the same depth, then each lot has the same width.
Step 1: Area of each lot = 44,000 sq. ft. ÷ 5 lots = 8,800 sq. ft. per lot
Step 2: Road frontage of each lot = 8,800 sq. ft. per lot ÷ 110 ft. = 80 ft. per lot

3. C
Conversion factor: 1 sq. mi. = 640 acres
Lot size = 640 acres × 0.19 = 121.6 acres

4. A
Step 1: Width of lot = 150,400 sq. ft. ÷ 820 ft. = 183.4146 ft.
Step 2: Selling price = $330 per ft. × 183.4146 ft. = $60,526.82

5. C
Conversion factor: 1 acre = 43,560 sq. ft.
Number of square feet = 3 acres × 43,560 sq. ft. per acre = 130,680 sq. ft.

6. B
Conversion factor: 1 acre = 43,560 sq. ft.
Step 1: Area of lot = 8.3 acres × 43,560 sq. ft. per acre = 361,548 sq. ft.
Step 2: Price per square foot = $1,785,000 ÷ 361,548 sq. ft. = $4.94 per sq. ft.

7. B
Conversion factor: 1 sq. mi. = 640 acres
Step 1: Area of land = 0.75 mi. × 0.75 mi. = 0.5625 sq. mi.
Step 2: Number of acres = 640 acres per sq. mi. × 0.5625 sq. mi. = 360 acres

8. D
Price per front foot = $201,500 ÷ 130 ft. = $1,550 per ft.

9. A
Conversion factor: 1 acre = 43,560 sq. ft.
Step 1: Area of land = 2,250 ft. × 2,925 ft. = 6,581,250 sq. ft.
Step 2: Number of acres = 6,581,250 sq. ft. ÷ 43,560 sq. ft. per acre = 151.08 acres

10. D
Conversion factor: 1 acre = 43,560 sq. ft.
Step 1: Area for drainage and other uses = 12.2 acres × 0.15 = 1.83 acres
Step 2: Remaining area for lots = 12.2 acres – 1.83 acres = 10.37 acres
Step 3: Square feet for lots = 10.37 acres × 43,560 sq. ft. per acre = 451,717.2 sq. ft.
Step 4: Number of lots = 451,717.2 sq. ft. ÷ 6,500 sq. ft. per lot = 69.5 = 69 full lots

11. D
Conversion factor 1: 1 section = 1 mi. × 1 mi.
Conversion factor 2: 1 mi. = 5,280 ft.
Area of a section = 5,280 ft. × 5,280 ft. = 27,878,400 sq. ft.

12. B
Conversion factor: 1 acre = 43,560 sq. ft.
Step 1: Area of land = 22.5 acres × 43,560 sq. ft. per acre = 980,100 sq. ft.
Step 2: Depth of land = 980,100 sq. ft. ÷ 865 ft. = 1,133.06 ft. = 1,133 ft. (rounded)

13. A
Conversion factor: 1 acre = 43,560 sq. ft.
Step 1: Area of land = 1,150 ft. × 2,050 ft. = 2,357,500 sq. ft.
Step 2: Number of acres = 2,357,500 sq. ft. ÷ 43,560 sq. ft. per acre = 54.1208 acres
Step 3: Price per acre = $950,000 ÷ 54.1208 acres = $17,533.33 per acre

14. C
Conversion factor: 1 acre = 43,560 sq. ft.
Step 1: Required square feet per lot = 15,000 sq. ft. + 1,750 sq. ft. = 16,750 sq. ft. per lot
Step 2: Area of lots = 425 lots × 16,750 sq. ft. per lot = 7,118,750 sq. ft.
Step 3: Number of acres = 7,118,750 sq. ft. ÷ 43,560 sq. ft. per acre = 163.42 acres

15. C
1 quadrangle = 24 mi. × 24 mi. = 576 sq. mi.

16. B
Conversion factor: 1 acre = 43,560 sq. ft.
Step 1: Area of land = 15 acres × 43,560 sq. ft. per acre = 653,400 sq. ft.
Step 2: Area of each lot = 225 ft. × 300 ft. = 67,500 sq. ft. per lot
Step 3: Number of lots = 653,400 sq. ft. ÷ 67,500 sq. ft. per lot = 9.68 = 9 full lots

17. D
Conversion factor: 1 sq. mi. = 640 acres
Percentage of a square mile = 78.5 acres ÷ 640 acres = 0.1227 = 12.27%

18. C
Conversion factor: 1 township = 36 sq. mi.
Step 1: Area of land = 12 mi. × 12 mi. = 144 sq. mi.
Step 2: Number of townships = 144 sq. mi. ÷ 36 sq. mi. per township = 4 townships

19. D
Conversion factor: 1 acre = 43,560 sq. ft.
Step 1: Cost of lot = 2 acres × 43,560 sq. ft. per acre × $6.15 per sq. ft. = $535,788.00
Step 2: Area of house = 85 ft. × 85 ft. = 7,225 sq. ft.
Step 3: Cost of house = 7,225 sq. ft. × $110.50 per sq. ft. = $798,362.50
Step 4: Total cost = $535,788.00 + $798,362.50 = $1,334,150.50

20. D
Conversion factor: 1 sq. mi. = 640 acres
Number of acres = 2.5 sq. mi. × 640 acres per sq. mi. = 1,600 acres

21. B
Step 1: Cost of house = 3,450 sq. ft. × $140.50 per sq. ft. = $484,725.00
Step 2: Cost of lot = 1.85 acres × $38,250 per acre = $70,762.50
Step 3: Total cost = $484,725.00 + $70,762.50 = $555,487.50

22. B
Step 1: Area for sidewalks and drainage = 32 acres × 0.25 = 8 acres
Step 2: Remaining area for lots = 32 acres – 8 acres = 24 acres
Step 3: Number of lots = 24 acres × 3 lots per acre = 72 lots

23. C
Step 1: Area for sidewalks and drainage = 32 acres × 0.25 = 8 acres
Step 2: Remaining area for lots = 32 acres – 8 acres = 24 acres
Step 3: Number of lots = 24 acres × 3 lots per acre = 72 lots
Step 4: Gross sales price = 72 lots × $35,500 per lot = $2,556,000

24. A
Step 1: Area for sidewalks and drainage = 32 acres × 0.25 = 8 acres
Step 2: Remaining area for lots = 32 acres – 8 acres = 24 acres
Step 3: Number of lots = 24 acres × 3 lots per acre = 72 lots
Step 4: Gross sales price = 72 lots × $35,500 per lot = $2,556,000
Step 5: Overhead and selling costs = $2,556,000 × 0.32 = $817,920

25. C
Step 1: Area for sidewalks and drainage = 32 acres × 0.25 = 8 acres
Step 2: Remaining area for lots = 32 acres – 8 acres = 24 acres
Step 3: Number of lots = 24 acres × 3 lots per acre = 72 lots
Step 4: Gross sales price = 72 lots × $35,500 per lot = $2,556,000
Step 5: Overhead and selling costs = $2,556,000 × 0.32 = $817,920
Step 6: Potential profit = $2,556,000 – $817,920 = $1,738,080

26. D
Conversion factor 1: 1 township = 36 sq. mi.
Conversion factor 2: 1 sq. mi. = 640 acres
Number of acres = 36 sq. mi. × 640 acres per sq. mi. = 23,040 acres

27. B
Conversion factor: 1 mi. = 5,280 ft.
Area of property = (5,280 ft. ÷ 2) × (5,280 ft. ÷ 2) = 6,969,600 sq. ft.

28. B
Conversion factor 1: 1 section = 1 mi. × 1 mi.
Conversion factor 2: 1 mi. = 5,280 ft.
Conversion factor 3: 1 acre = 43,560 sq. ft.
Step 1: Area of section (in square feet) = 5,280 ft. × 5,280 ft. = 27,878,400 sq. ft.
Step 2: Area of section (in acres) = 27,878,400 sq. ft. ÷ 43,560 sq. ft. per acre = 640 acres
Step 3: Total area = 3 sections × 640 acres per section = 1,920 acres

29. A
Conversion factor 1: 1 section = 640 acres
Conversion factor 2: 1 acre = 43,560 sq. ft.
Step 1: Area of land (in acres) = 640 acres × ½ × ¼ × ¼ × ¼ = 5 acres
Step 2: Area of land (in square feet) = 5 acres × 43,560 sq. ft. per acre = 217,800 sq. ft.

30. D
In the Public Land Survey System, a township has 36 sections.

31. C
Conversion factor: 1 acre = 43,560 sq. ft.
Step 1: Area of land = 18 acres × 43,560 sq. ft. per acre = 784,080 sq. ft.
Step 2: Remaining area for lots = 784,080 sq. ft. – 232,830 sq. ft. = 551,250 sq. ft.
Step 3: Area of each lot = 90 ft. × 125 ft. = 11,250 sq. ft. per lot
Step 4: Number of lots = 551,250 sq. ft. ÷ 11,250 sq. ft. per lot = 49 lots

32. D
Conversion factor: 1 acre = 43,560 sq. ft.
Step 1: Area of land = 18 acres × 43,560 sq. ft. per acre = 784,080 sq. ft.
Step 2: Remaining area for lots = 784,080 sq. ft. – 232,830 sq. ft. = 551,250 sq. ft.
Step 3: Area of each lot = 90 ft. × 125 ft. = 11,250 sq. ft. per lot
Step 4: Number of lots = 551,250 sq. ft. ÷ 11,250 sq. ft. per lot = 49 lots
Step 5: Price per lot = $1,715,000 ÷ 49 lots = $35,000 per lot

33. B
Conversion factor 1: 1 mi. = 5,280 ft.
Conversion factor 2: 1 acre = 43,560 sq. ft.
Step 1: Area of lot (in square feet) = (5,280 ft. ÷ 3) × (5,280 ft. ÷ 6) = 1,548,800 sq. ft.
Step 2: Area of lot (in acres) = 1,548,800 sq. ft. ÷ 43,560 sq. ft. per acre = 35.56 acres

34. A
Step 1: Area for roads = 64 acres × 0.165 = 10.56 acres
Step 2: Remaining area for lots = 64 acres – 10.56 acres = 53.44 acres
Step 3: Number of lots = 53.44 acres ÷ 1 acre per lot = 53.44 = 53 full lots
Step 4: Price per lot = $1,033,500 ÷ 53 lots = $19,500 per lot

35. D
Step 1: Area of each lot = 75 ft. × 165 ft. = 12,375 sq. ft. per lot
Step 2: Total area = 12,375 sq. ft. per lot × 5 lots = 61,875 sq. ft.
Step 3: Price per square foot = $142,900 ÷ 61,875 sq. ft. = $2.31 per sq. ft.

SECTION 2

AGENCY AGREEMENTS AND COMMISSIONS

QUESTIONS

1. Caitlin, a listing broker, will receive a commission of 6.5% on the first $300,000 of a property's sale price, and 4.5% on any amount over $300,000. If a property sells for $725,000, Caitlin's commission will be:

   A. $32,910.
   B. $33,800.
   C. $36,050.
   D. $38,625.

2. A 60-acre property sold for $17,000 per acre with a 6% commission. If the listing broker and selling broker will split the commission evenly, each broker will receive:

   A. $15,300.
   B. $30,600.
   C. $45,900.
   D. $61,200.

3. John's house was listed for $550,000 and sold for $525,000. If the listing broker split the 5% commission evenly with the selling broker, the listing broker's commission was:

   A. $13,125.
   B. $13,750.
   C. $26,250.
   D. $27,500.

4. The Smith's farm was listed for $480,000 and sold for $440,000. The Smith's closing costs were 2.5%, and the broker's commission was 5.5%. If the mortgage balance at the time of the sale was $195,000, the Smiths received _____ in cash at closing.

   A. $200,600
   B. $209,800
   C. $228,500
   D. $246,600

The following information relates to questions 5 – 6.
Katherine recently sold her house and received a check for $92,375 after paying $3,000 of closing costs and a 5% commission.

5. Based on the information provided, the gross sales price of Katherine's house was:

   A. $95,375.
   B. $96,994.
   C. $99,994.
   D. $100,395.

6. Based on the information provided, the commission was:

    A. $4,769.25.
    B. $4,850.50.
    C. $5,000.00.
    D. $5,019.75.

7. Dustin, a salesperson, is required to pay $750 per month to the broker for use of office space, and he receives 50% of commissions brought in. Last month, if Dustin received a net payment of $2,200, the amount of commissions that he collected was:

    A. $1,100.
    B. $2,450.
    C. $2,950.
    D. $5,900.

8. A property sold for $650,000 with a 5% commission. The listing broker paid the selling broker 50%. The listing salesperson and the selling salesperson each received 50% of what their brokers received. The selling salesperson received:

    A. $4,063.
    B. $8,125.
    C. $16,250.
    D. $32,500.

9. Carolyn, a broker, listed a property for $515,000 at a 7% commission rate. If the eventual sales price was $493,400, her commission was _____ less than it would have been if the property had sold at the listed price.

    A. $1,512
    B. $2,268
    C. $3,024
    D. $21,600

10. Alexander, a salesperson, receives 40% of the first $75,000 of commissions he brings in, and 50% of the amount in excess of $75,000. If his real estate sales totaled $2,600,000 last year, and he received a 6% commission on all sales, then Alexander received a payout of:

    A. $64,500.
    B. $68,500.
    C. $70,500.
    D. $75,000.

The following information relates to questions 11 – 12.
Peter, a salesperson, works for a broker. Peter receives 45% of all commissions that he brings in. He recently sold a house for $335,200 at a 5% commission rate.

11. Based on the information provided, Peter's share of the proceeds is:

    A. $7,542.
    B. $8,380.
    C. $9,218.
    D. $10,056.

12. Based on the information provided, the broker's share of the proceeds is:

    A. $7,542.
    B. $8,380.
    C. $9,218.
    D. $10,056.

13. Lydia sold her house and paid a 6% commission and 2.5% of the selling price in closing costs. If she received $285,480, the gross sales price of her house was:

    A. $303,000.
    B. $312,000.
    C. $315,000.
    D. $321,000.

14. Eric, a broker with a 5% commission rate, is determining the ideal listing price for his client's house. If the value of the lot is $160,000 net of commission, and the value of the house is $368,000 net of commission, the listing price should be:

    A. $546,193.
    B. $549,371.
    C. $552,813.
    D. $555,789.

The following information relates to questions 15 – 16.
Greg referred a client to Patty, who sold the client a house for $659,000. Patty paid Greg a referral fee equal to 9% of her commission. Greg received $3,558.60 from Patty.

15. Based on the information provided, Patty's commission was:

    A. $3,879.
    B. $39,540.
    C. $49,425.
    D. $59,310.

16. Based on the information provided, Patty's commission rate was:

    A. 4%.
    B. 5%.
    C. 6%.
    D. 7%.

17. Deb, a broker, sold an office building for $425,300. If her commission rate was 7% and she received 65% of the total sales commission, her payout was:

    A. $19,351.15.
    B. $19,460.18.
    C. $19,576.24.
    D. $19,804.35.

18. If Dean is selling his house and wants to net $265,000 from the sale after paying a 6% commission, his house must sell for:

    A. $280,900.
    B. $281,915.
    C. $282,225.
    D. $283,040.

19. A broker pays his salesperson, Kim, 45% of commissions up to $150,000 of commissions received each year, and 55% of commissions in excess of $150,000. If Kim generated $329,500 in total gross commissions, she will earn:

    A. $98,725.
    B. $135,000.
    C. $145,865.
    D. $166,225.

20. Jim, a broker, has a listing that requires a 5% brokerage commission. Jim offers 40% of the commission to the selling broker, Wendy. If Jim sells the property for $525,650, the seller must pay him:

    A. $10,513.00.
    B. $13,141.25.
    C. $21,026.00.
    D. $26,282.50.

21. After paying a 4.5% commission, Adam received net proceeds of $422,587.50 from the sale of his house. The gross sales price was:

    A. $434,300.
    B. $442,500.
    C. $444,100.
    D. $445,300.

22. Rob, a broker, has agreed to pay his salesperson one-fourth of all commissions earned as a result of the salesperson's efforts. If the salesperson sells a property for $950,000 with a 4% commission rate, then Rob's share of the commission is:

    A. $9,500.
    B. $28,500.
    C. $30,000.
    D. $38,000.

23. Christie, a broker, shares the commission that is earned on the sale of real estate with her salesperson in a 4 to 3 ratio, respectively. If the salesperson sells a property for $299,000 at a 6% commission rate, then Christie will earn _____ more than the sales-person.

    A. $2,562.86
    B. $2,730.53
    C. $2,819.47
    D. $2,993.19

24. Vaughn would like to net $155,000 from the sale of his house. If his closing costs will be $14,200, and the broker's commission rate is 6%, the gross sales price of his house should be:

    A. $150,000.
    B. $160,000.
    C. $170,000.
    D. $180,000.

25. Daniel purchased a property for $270,000. Two years later, he sold the property for $305,000 and paid a broker's commission of 5%. Daniel's rate of profit after paying the commission was:

    A. 6.47%.
    B. 7.31%.
    C. 9.53%.
    D. 12.96%.

26. Kelly, a broker, will receive a commission of 6% on the first $75,000 of a property's sale price, 4.5% on the next $75,000, and 2.5% for the remainder. If Kelly sells her client's house for $390,000, her commission will be:

    A. $13,675.
    B. $13,875.
    C. $14,050.
    D. $14,205.

The following information relates to questions 27 – 28.
A broker keeps 60% of sales commissions and pays her salesperson the remaining 40%. Last month the salesperson sold 35 acres of land at $1,400 per acre, with a gross commission rate of 8%.

27. Based on the information provided, the broker earned:

    A. $1,284.
    B. $1,568.
    C. $2,352.
    D. $3,920.

28. Based on the information provided, the salesperson earned:

    A. $1,284.
    B. $1,568.
    C. $2,352.
    D. $3,920.

29. Travis received $185,000 from the sale of his house. If he paid $9,500 in closing costs in addition to a 5.5% commission, the gross sales price of his house was:

    A. $185,714.
    B. $195,767.
    C. $205,198.
    D. $205,820.

30. Monica, a broker, sold her client's house for $2,095,500. If her commission rate was 5.5%, her commission was:

    A. $104,750.00.
    B. $104,775.50.
    C. $115,225.00.
    D. $115,252.50.

31. Angela sold her client's house for $225,000, which represents a 10% decrease from the original listing price. If Angela receives 7% of the final sale price, she would have earned _____ if the house had sold for its original price.

    A. $12,250
    B. $17,500
    C. $18,750
    D. $22,500

32. Corey, a broker, sold his client's house and received a 6% commission, which was equal to $14,700. The gross sales price of the house was:

A. $225,000.
B. $235,000.
C. $245,000.
D. $255,000.

The following information relates to questions 33 – 34.

A salesperson associated with a broker listed a house for $485,000 with a 5.5% commission. A month later, the homeowner accepted an offer of $460,000, brought in by the salesperson. The broker's practice is that 40% of commissions are retained by the office and the remainder is paid to the salesperson.

33. Based on the information provided, the salesperson's payout will be:

A. $10,120.
B. $10,670.
C. $15,180.
D. $16,005.

34. Based on the information provided, the office will retain:

A. $10,120.
B. $10,670.
C. $15,180.
D. $16,005.

35. Carl, a salesperson, receives 55% of the total commission on a property that sold for $210,000. If he received $6,930, his rate of commission was:

A. 5%.
B. 6%.
C. 7%.
D. 8%.

ANSWER KEY

1. D
Step 1: Commission on the first $300,000 = $300,000 × 0.065 = $19,500
Step 2: Commission over $300,000 = ($725,000 – $300,000) × 0.045 = $19,125
Step 3: Total commission = $19,500 + $19,125 = $38,625

2. B
Step 1: Total sales price = 60 acres × $17,000 per acre = $1,020,000
Step 2: Total commission = $1,020,000 × 0.06 = $61,200
Step 3: Each broker's commission = $61,200 × 0.5 = $30,600

3. A
Step 1: Total commission = $525,000 × 0.05 = $26,250
Step 2: Listing broker's commission = $26,250 × 0.5 = $13,125

4. B
Step 1: Closing costs = $440,000 × 0.025 = $11,000
Step 2: Broker's commission = $440,000 × 0.055 = $24,200
Step 3: Equity in farm = $440,000 – $195,000 = $245,000
Step 4: Cash received at closing = $245,000 – $11,000 – $24,200 = $209,800

5. D
Gross sales price = ($92,375 + $3,000) ÷ (1 – 0.05) = $100,395

6. D
Step 1: Gross sales price = ($92,375 + $3,000) ÷ (1 – 0.05) = $100,395
Step 2: Commission = $100,395 × 0.05 = $5,019.75

7. C
Commission collected = $2,200 + $750 = $2,950

8. B
Step 1: Total commission = $650,000 × 0.05 = $32,500
Step 2: Broker's payout = $32,500 × 0.5 = $16,250
Step 3: Salesperson's payout = $16,250 × 0.5 = $8,125

9. A
Step 1: List price commission = $515,000 × 0.07 = $36,050
Step 2: Sale price commission = $493,400 × 0.07 = $34,538
Step 3: Difference = $36,050 – $34,538 = $1,512

10. C
Step 1: Total commission = $2,600,000 × 0.06 = $156,000
Step 2: Payout on the first $75,000 = $75,000 × 0.4 = $30,000
Step 3: Payout on amount over $75,000 = ($156,000 – $75,000) × 0.5 = $40,500
Step 4: Total payout = $30,000 + $40,500 = $70,500

11. A
Step 1: Total commission = $335,200 × 0.05 = $16,760
Step 2: Salesperson's payout = $16,760 × 0.45 = $7,542

12. C
Step 1: Total commission = $335,200 × 0.05 = $16,760
Step 2: Broker's payout = $16,760 × (1 – 0.45) = $9,218

13. B
Gross sales price = $285,480 ÷ (1 – 0.06 – 0.025) = $312,000

14. D
Listing price = ($160,000 + $368,000) ÷ (1 – 0.05) = $555,789

15. B
Patty's commission = $3,558.60 ÷ 0.09 = $39,540

16. C
Step 1: Patty's commission = $3,558.60 ÷ 0.09 = $39,540
Step 2: Patty's commission rate = $39,540 ÷ $659,000 = 0.06 = 6%

17. A
Step 1: Total commission: $425,300 × 0.07 = $29,771
Step 2: Broker's payout: $29,771 × 0.65 = $19,351.15

18. B
Sale price = $265,000 ÷ (1 – 0.06) = $281,915

19. D
Step 1: Payout on the first $150,000 = $150,000 × 0.45 = $67,500
Step 2: Payout on amount over $150,000 = ($329,500 – $150,000) × 0.55 = $98,725
Step 3: Total payout = $67,500 + $98,725 = $166,225

20. D
Broker's commission = $525,650 × 0.05 = $26,282.50

21. B
Gross sales price = $422,587.50 ÷ (1 – 0.045) = $442,500

22. B
Step 1: Total commission = $950,000 × 0.04 = $38,000
Step 2: Broker's commission = $38,000 × 0.75 = $28,500
(The remaining $9,500 will be paid to the salesperson.)

23. A
Step 1: Total commission = $299,000 × 0.06 = $17,940
Step 2: Broker's payout = $17,940 × 4/7 = $10,251.43
Step 3: Salesperson's payout = $17,940 × 3/7 = $7,688.57
Step 4: Difference = $10,251.43 – $7,688.57 = $2,562.86

24. D
Gross sales price = ($155,000 + $14,200) ÷ (1 – 0.06) = $180,000

25. B
Step 1: Net sale price = $305,000 × (1 – 0.05) = $289,750
Step 2: Rate of profit = ($289,750 – $270,000) ÷ $270,000 = 0.0731 = 7.31%

26. B
Step 1: Commission on the first $75,000 = $75,000 × 0.06 = $4,500
Step 2: Commission on the next $75,000 = $75,000 × 0.045 = $3,375
Step 3: Commission over $150,000 = ($390,000 – $150,000) × 0.025 = $6,000
Step 4: Total commission = $4,500 + $3,375 + $6,000 = $13,875

27. C
Step 1: Total sales price = 35 acres × $1,400 per acre = $49,000
Step 2: Total commission = $49,000 × 0.08 = $3,920
Step 3: Broker's payout = $3,920 × 0.6 = $2,352

28. B
Step 1: Total sales price = 35 acres × $1,400 per acre = $49,000
Step 2: Total commission = $49,000 × 0.08 = $3,920
Step 3: Salesperson's payout = $3,920 × 0.4 = $1,568

29. D
Gross sales price = ($185,000 + $9,500) ÷ (1 – 0.055) = $205,820

30. D
Commission = $2,095,500 × 0.055 = $115,252.50

31. B
Step 1: Original listing price = $225,000 ÷ (1 – 0.1) = $250,000
Step 2: Commission = $250,000 × 0.07 = $17,500

32. C
Gross sales price = $14,700 ÷ 0.06 = $245,000

33. C
Step 1: Total commission = $460,000 × 0.055 = $25,300
Step 2: Salesperson's payout = $25,300 × (1 – 0.4) = $15,180

34. A
Step 1: Total commission = $460,000 × 0.055 = $25,300
Step 2: Earnings retained by office = $25,300 × 0.4 = $10,120

35. B
Step 1: Salesperson's commission = $6,930 ÷ 0.55 = $12,600
Step 2: Salesperson's commission rate = $12,600 ÷ $210,000 = 0.06 = 6%

SECTION 3

MORTGAGES AND FINANCE

QUESTIONS

1. Alpha Mortgage Company's underwriting requirements specify a maximum housing debt-to-income ratio of 28%. If the applicant discloses annual earnings of $75,000, the maximum monthly PITI payment the mortgage company will accept is:

A. $1,750.
B. $1,825.
C. $6,250.
D. $21,000.

2. The seller has agreed to pay 1.5 points to the mortgage company to help the buyer obtain a mortgage. The house was listed for $725,000 and is being sold for $695,000. If the buyer will pay 15% in cash and borrow the remaining amount, the seller will owe _____ to the lender for points.

A. $8,861.25
B. $9,243.75
C. $10,425.00
D. $10,875.00

3. Amanda is selling her house and the closing date is July 24, 2017. Interest is payable, with the payment on the 15th of the month. The loan amount as of July 15, 2017, is $185,400. The annual interest rate is 4.85%. If the loan is assumed, Amanda will have to pay the buyer _____ in prorated interest.

A. $230.18
B. $234.86
C. $241.72
D. $255.18

4. Diana has an annual income of $95,000. A mortgage lender will provide a loan equal to 2.5 times annual income. If Diana makes a 20% down payment, the maximum house that she can afford to purchase is:

A. $190,000.
B. $237,500.
C. $284,425.
D. $296,875.

5. If mortgage interest for the current month is $610, and the interest rate is 4.75%, then the principal balance is:

A. $148,390.65.
B. $154,106.56.
C. $158,126.60.
D. $164,975.50.

6. Ken's mortgage balance is $300,000 and carries a 4% interest rate. If monthly payments are $1,500, the principal will be reduced by _____ by the second payment.

    A. $500
    B. $502
    C. $504
    D. $506

7. Two discount points is equal to:

    A. 2% of the loan amount.
    B. 2% of the sale price.
    C. 2% of the interest rate.
    D. 2% of the property value.

8. Nicole owns a warehouse with a current value of $185,000. Justin owns a building with a current value of $350,000 and a $40,000 mortgage balance. If Nicole assumes the mortgage, a fair trade would require:

    A. Nicole to pay $125,000 cash.
    B. Nicole to pay $225,000 cash.
    C. Justin to pay $125,000 cash.
    D. Justin to pay $225,000 cash.

9. If Randy's mortgage balance is $230,000 and requires a payment of $4,600 each quarter in interest, the annual interest rate is:

    A. 7.0%.
    B. 7.5%.
    C. 8.0%.
    D. 8.5%.

10. Sarah would like to purchase a building for $1,200,000. If she pays $50,000 in earnest money and applies for a mortgage equal to 80% of the purchase price, then she will need to pay _____ to meet the requirements of the loan.

    A. $50,000
    B. $190,000
    C. $230,000
    D. $290,000

11. Kay's mortgage carries an interest rate of 4.25%. If the interest payable for the current month is $1,243.66, the mortgage balance at the beginning of the month was:

    A. $351,147.75.
    B. $353,425.78.
    C. $357,981.80.
    D. $359,610.37.

12. Lewis is purchasing a condo for $358,900. If the mortgage requires a 10% down payment, a 0.5% private mortgage insurance (PMI) fee, and a 0.9% origination fee, the total amount that Lewis will have to pay is:

  A. $34,082.33.
  B. $36,540.29.
  C. $38,638.76.
  D. $40,412.14.

13. Mark acquired a 20-year mortgage with a beginning balance of $247,350. If the interest rate is 4.65% and monthly payments are $1,584.96, then the total interest paid if the mortgage runs to maturity is:

  A. $127,478.47.
  B. $133,040.40.
  C. $138,582.70.
  D. $143,019.34.

The following information relates to questions 14 – 15.
Barbara has a 30-year mortgage with a current balance of $240,000 and an interest rate of 5.5%. Her house was recently appraised for $320,000.

14. Based on the information provided, the equity in Barbara's house is:

  A. $80,000.
  B. $185,000.
  C. $275,000.
  D. $460,000.

15. Based on the information provided, Barbara's debt-to-equity ratio is:

  A. 1:4.
  B. 1:3.
  C. 3:1.
  D. 4:1.

16. Phil obtained an interest-only mortgage with a balance of $300,000 and a 6% interest rate. The term of the mortgage is 30 years, including the interest-only period of 7 years. The amount of interest Phil will have paid after the first 3 months of the mortgage is:

  A. $4,239.31.
  B. $4,434.83.
  C. $4,486.23.
  D. $4,500.00.

17. Linda purchased a house for $814,000 and obtained a mortgage for 90% of the purchase price. If the mortgage fee is 1.25%, Linda must pay:

A. $9,151.70.
B. $9,154.30.
C. $9,157.50.
D. $9,162.80.

18. Anthony acquired a 15-year mortgage in the amount of $250,000. If the interest rate is 4.8%, the principal balance after the first monthly payment of $1,951.04 is:

A. $248,912.14.
B. $249,048.96.
C. $249,224.36.
D. $249,308.28.

The following information relates to questions 19 – 20.
Laurie obtained a 20-year mortgage with a current balance of $140,000. The interest rate on the mortgage is 6% and monthly payments are $1,003.00.

19. Based on the information provided, the interest payment in the first month will be:

A. $694.10.
B. $700.00.
C. $703.20.
D. $706.00.

20. Based on the information provided, the principal payment in the first month will be:

A. $303.00.
B. $304.12.
C. $306.00.
D. $308.94.

21. Jose obtained a 30-year mortgage with a balance of $60,000. If the interest rate is 5.25%, the first month's interest payment will be:

A. $258.25.
B. $260.00.
C. $262.50.
D. $264.50.

22. Carol has a mortgage with a current balance of $613,564. If the monthly payment is $3,849, and the house was recently appraised for $902,300, the loan-to-value ratio is:

A. 62%.
B. 64%.
C. 66%.
D. 68%.

23. Pamela is purchasing a house for $275,000. If she's made an earnest money deposit of $4,000, and the lender has agreed to provide a mortgage equal to 70% of the sale price, the amount of additional cash that she must pay in order to meet the requirements of the loan is:

A. $74,500.
B. $76,500.
C. $78,500.
D. $86,500.

24. Maria obtained a loan in the amount of $592,300. If the annual interest rate is 4.625%, the amount of interest that she will owe in the first year is:

A. $2,282.82.
B. $19,210.83.
C. $26,482.34.
D. $27,393.88.

25. Paul is purchasing a house with a current value of $710,000. If he will acquire a mortgage equal to 85% of the house value, and he has already paid $14,750 in earnest money, then he must pay _____ to meet the requirements of the loan.

A. $91,750
B. $92,500
C. $93,250
D. $95,500

26. Andrew acquires a 15-year mortgage with a balance of $180,000. If the interest rate is 6%, and he pays back the mortgage using level principal payments each month, the payment for the first month will be:

A. $1,700.
B. $1,800.
C. $1,900.
D. $2,000.

27. Alex obtained a 30-year mortgage in the amount of $340,000. If the interest rate is 5.5% and monthly payments are $1,930.48, the total interest paid over the life of the mortgage is:

A. $340,000.00.
B. $354,972.80.
C. $356,270.73.
D. $358,389.34.

28. If Tom's annual income is $38,000, then his monthly mortgage payment of $1,400 represents _____ of his annual income.

    A. 3.7%
    B. 28.6%
    C. 44.2%
    D. 55.8%

29. If the first month's interest payment on a mortgage is $612.50, and the interest rate is 7.5%, the mortgage balance is:

    A. $97,000.
    B. $98,000.
    C. $99,000.
    D. $100,000.

30. Kathleen is purchasing a property for $372,000 and is applying for a mortgage. If the lender requires an 80% loan-to-value ratio, Kathleen's down payment will need to be:

    A. $74,400.
    B. $75,800.
    C. $76,200.
    D. $77,500.

31. Marcia is obtaining a mortgage with closing costs equal to 1.75 discount points. If the property is valued at $220,000, and the mortgage is 85% of the property's value, then Marcia must pay closing costs of:

    A. $3,080.90.
    B. $3,120.40.
    C. $3,190.25.
    D. $3,272.50.

The following information relates to questions 32 – 35.
Karen purchased a house for $160,000 and obtained a mortgage in the amount of $120,000. The interest rate on the mortgage is 5% and the monthly payment is $700.

32. Based on the information provided, the amount of interest that will be paid during the first year is:

    A. $500.
    B. $6,000.
    C. $8,424.
    D. $17,550.

33. Based on the information provided, the amount of interest that will be paid in the first month is:

    A. $0.
    B. $200.
    C. $500.
    D. $700.

34. Based on the information provided, the amount of principal that will be paid in the first month is:

    A. $0.
    B. $200.
    C. $500.
    D. $700.

35. Based on the information provided, the loan balance after the first month's payment will be:

    A. $119,600.
    B. $119,800.
    C. $119,850.
    D. $119,900.

36. Patrick is purchasing a house for $425,000. If the appraised value is $390,000, and the bank offers an 80% loan-to-value ratio, his required down payment will be:

    A. $35,000.
    B. $78,000.
    C. $85,000.
    D. $113,000.

37. James has an annual income of $118,000. If he wants to keep his PITI payments at or below 28% of his income, and he also wants to keep his total debt payments at or below 36% of his income, the maximum monthly PITI payment that he can afford is:

    A. $2,103.65.
    B. $2,457.82.
    C. $2,753.33.
    D. $3,540.00.

38. If Stacey borrows $224,000 and pays $5,600 semiannually in interest, then the annual interest rate on the loan is:

    A. 3.5%.
    B. 4.0%.
    C. 4.5%.
    D. 5.0%.

39. The seller has agreed to pay 3 points to the mortgage company to help the buyer obtain a mortgage. If the house is being sold for $540,000, and the buyer will pay 20% in cash and borrow the remaining amount, the seller will owe _____ to the lender for points.

    A. $11,480
    B. $12,960
    C. $13,530
    D. $14,410

40. Carrie has an annual income of $100,000. She is applying for a mortgage, and the lender will provide a loan up to 3 times annual income. If Carrie makes a 20% down payment, the maximum house that she can afford to purchase is:

    A. $375,000.
    B. $380,000.
    C. $385,000.
    D. $390,000.

ANSWER KEY

1. A
Step 1: Maximum annual PITI = $75,000 × 0.28 = $21,000
Step 2: Maximum monthly PITI = $21,000 ÷ 12 months = $1,750

2. A
Step 1: Mortgage amount = $695,000 × (1 – 0.15) = $590,750
Step 2: Amount seller will owe for points = $590,750 × 0.015 = $8,861.25

3. C
Step 1: Monthly interest payable = $185,400 ÷ 12 months × 0.0485 = $749.325
Step 2: Daily interest payable = $749.325 ÷ 31 days = $24.172
Step 3: The seller owned the property for 10 days.
Step 4: Amount of interest seller owes buyer = $24.172 × 10 days = $241.72

4. D
Step 1: Maximum mortgage = $95,000 × 2.5 = $237,500
Step 2: Maximum purchase price = $237,500 ÷ (1 – 0.2) = $296,875

5. B
Step 1: Monthly interest rate = 0.0475 ÷ 12 months = 0.0039583
Step 2: Mortgage balance = $610 ÷ 0.0039583 = $154,106.56

6. B
Step 1: Annual interest = $300,000 × 0.04 = $12,000
Step 2: Monthly interest = $12,000 ÷ 12 months = $1,000
Step 3: Principal reduction from first payment = $1,500 – $1,000 = $500
Step 4: New mortgage balance = $300,000 – $500 = $299,500
Step 5: New annual interest = $299,500 × 0.04 = $11,980
Step 6: New monthly interest = $11,980 ÷ 12 months = $998
Step 7: Principal reduction from second payment: $1,500 – $998 = $502

7. A
Two discount points is equal to 2% of the loan amount.

8. A
Step 1: Nicole's equity before trade = $185,000
Step 2: Justin's equity before trade = $350,000 – $40,000 = $310,000
Step 3: Difference in equity = $310,000 – $185,000 = $125,000; A fair trade requires Nicole to pay Justin $125,000.

9. C
Step 1: Annual interest payment = $4,600 × 4 quarters = $18,400
Step 2: Annual interest rate = $18,400 ÷ $230,000 = 0.08 = 8%

10. B
Step 1: Down payment = $1,200,000 × (1 – 0.8) = $240,000
Step 2: Additional cash required = $240,000 – $50,000 = $190,000

11. A
Step 1: Monthly interest rate = 0.0425 ÷ 12 months = 0.0035417
Step 2: Mortgage balance = $1,243.66 ÷ 0.0035417 = $351,147.75

12. D
Step 1: Down payment = $358,900 × 0.1 = $35,890
Step 2: Mortgage amount = $358,900 – $35,890 = $323,010
Step 3: PMI fee = $323,010 × 0.005 = $1,615.05
Step 4: Origination fee = $323,010 × 0.009 = $2,907.09
Step 5: Total amount due = $35,890 + $1,615.05 + $2,907.09 = $40,412.14

13. B
Step 1: Number of payments = 20 years × 12 months = 240
Step 2: Total amount of payments = 240 × $1,584.96 = $380,390.40
Step 3: Total interest paid = $380,390.40 – $247,350.00 = $133,040.40

14. A
Owner's equity = $320,000 – $240,000 = $80,000

15. C
Step 1: Owner's equity = $320,000 – $240,000 = $80,000
Step 2: Debt-to-equity = $240,000 ÷ $80,000 = 3:1

16. D
Step 1: Monthly interest rate = 0.06 ÷ 12 months = 0.005
Step 2: Monthly interest = $300,000 × 0.005 = $1,500
Step 3: Total interest paid = $1,500 × 3 months = $4,500

17. C
Step 1: Mortgage amount = $814,000 × 0.9 = $732,600
Step 2: Mortgage fee = $732,600 × 0.0125 = $9,157.50

18. B
Step 1: Annual interest = $250,000 × 0.048 = $12,000
Step 2: Monthly interest = $12,000 ÷ 12 months = $1,000
Step 3: Principal reduction from first payment = $1,951.04 – $1,000.00 = $951.04
Step 4: New mortgage balance = $250,000 – $951.04 = $249,048.96

19. B
Step 1: Monthly interest rate = 0.06 ÷ 12 months = 0.005
Step 2: Monthly interest = $140,000 × 0.005 = $700

20. A
Step 1: Monthly interest rate = 0.06 ÷ 12 months = 0.005
Step 2: Monthly interest = $140,000 × 0.005 = $700
Step 3: Principal reduction from first payment = $1,003 – $700 = $303

21. C
Step 1: Annual interest = $60,000 × 0.0525 = $3,150
Step 2: Monthly interest = $3,150 ÷ 12 months = $262.50

22. D
Loan-to-value = $613,564 ÷ $902,300 = 0.68 = 68%

23. C
Step 1: Down payment = $275,000 × (1 – 0.7) = $82,500
Step 2: Additional cash required = $82,500 – $4,000 = $78,500

24. D
Annual interest = $592,300 × 0.04625 = $27,393.88

25. A
Step 1: Down payment = $710,000 × (1 – 0.85) = $106,500
Step 2: Additional cash required = $106,500 – $14,750 = $91,750

26. C
Step 1: Mortgage term = 15 years × 12 months = 180 months
Step 2: Monthly principal payment = $180,000 ÷ 180 months = $1,000
Step 3: Monthly interest rate = 0.06 ÷ 12 months = 0.005
Step 4: Monthly interest payment = $180,000 × 0.005 = $900
Step 5: Total monthly payment = $1,000 + $900 = $1,900

27. B
Step 1: Number of payments = 30 years × 12 months = 360
Step 2: Total amount of payments = 360 × $1,930.48 = $694,972.80
Step 3: Total interest paid = $694,972.80 – $340,000.00 = $354,972.80

28. C
Step 1: Annual mortgage payment = $1,400 × 12 months = $16,800
Step 2: Payment as a percent of income = $16,800 ÷ $38,000 = 0.442 = 44.2%

29. B
Step 1: Monthly interest rate = 0.075 ÷ 12 months = 0.00625
Step 2: Mortgage balance = $612.50 ÷ 0.00625 = $98,000

30. A
Step 1: Mortgage amount = $372,000 × 0.8 = $297,600
Step 2: Down payment = $372,000 – $297,600 = $74,400

31. D
Step 1: Mortgage amount = $220,000 × 0.85 = $187,000
Step 2: Closing costs = $187,000 × 0.0175 = $3,272.50

32. B
First year interest payment = $120,000 × 0.05 = $6,000

33. C
Step 1: First year interest payment = $120,000 × 0.05 = $6,000
Step 2: First month interest payment = $6,000 ÷ 12 months = $500

34. B
Step 1: First year interest payment = $120,000 × 0.05 = $6,000
Step 2: First month interest payment = $6,000 ÷ 12 months = $500
Step 3: First month principal payment = $700 – $500 = $200

35. B
Step 1: First year interest payment = $120,000 × 0.05 = $6,000
Step 2: First month interest payment = $6,000 ÷ 12 months = $500
Step 3: First month principal payment = $700 – $500 = $200
Step 4: Loan balance after first payment = $120,000 – $200 = $119,800

36. D
Step 1: Mortgage amount = $390,000 × 0.8 = $312,000
Step 2: Down payment = $425,000 – $312,000 = $113,000

37. C
Step 1: Maximum annual PITI payments = $118,000 × 0.28 = $33,040
Step 2: Maximum monthly PITI payments = $33,040 ÷ 12 months = $2,753.33

38. D
Step 1: Annual interest = $5,600 × 2 periods = $11,200
Step 2: Annual interest rate = $11,200 ÷ $224,000 = 0.05 = 5%

39. B
Step 1: Mortgage amount = $540,000 × (1 – 0.2) = $432,000
Step 2: Amount seller will owe for points = $432,000 × 0.03 = $12,960

40. A
Step 1: Maximum mortgage = $100,000 × 3 = $300,000
Step 2: Maximum purchase price = $300,000 ÷ (1 – 0.2) = $375,000

SECTION 4

APPRAISING REAL ESTATE VALUES

QUESTIONS

1. Helen's rental property produces annual gross income of $36,000. Expenses associated with the property are $12,000 per year. If the capitalization rate is 14%, the market value of her property is:

   A. $85,714.29.
   B. $171,428.57.
   C. $205,904.12.
   D. $257,142.86.

2. If a house that sold for $650,000 now rents for $51,600 per year, the monthly gross rent multiplier is:

   A. 12.60.
   B. 86.75.
   C. 112.85.
   D. 151.16.

3. Brad purchased an apartment building for $390,000. If he collects $3,200 per month in net operating income, the capitalization rate is:

   A. 9.85%.
   B. 9.92%.
   C. 10.03%.
   D. 10.12%.

4. If the appropriate time adjustment for a 10-acre farm is an increase of 4% per year compounded annually, then the time adjustment for a comparable farm that sold for $550,000 three years ago is:

   A. $44,880.00.
   B. $68,675.20.
   C. $80,949.60.
   D. $93,422.20.

5. Sigma Mortgage Company is estimating the value of a 14-year-old house measuring 45 feet by 55 feet. The original cost was $110 per square foot, and depreciation is estimated to be 2.5% per year. If the lot is valued at $95,000, the estimated total property value is:

   A. $176,962.50.
   B. $258,732.00.
   C. $271,962.50.
   D. $367,250.00.

6. If the gross rent multiplier is 85, and Richard's property rents for $180,000 per year, the value of his property is:

   A. $2,117.
   B. $333,000.
   C. $15,300,000.
   D. $19,800,000.

7. The current value of Dawn's house, excluding the lot, is $255,000. If her house has depreciated 4.5% per year for the past 6 years, the original value of her house was:

   A. $186,150.00.
   B. $266,675.00.
   C. $290,322.58.
   D. $349,315.07.

8. If comparable properties have been appreciating by 8% per year, a house that sold for $195,000 three years ago would be worth _____ today.

   A. $236,395.17
   B. $239,491.92
   C. $242,582.45
   D. $245,643.84

9. Gregory's house sustained damage in a recent hurricane. If the house was worth $480,000 before the storm, and a 35% loss was sustained, the value of his house after the storm is:

   A. $168,000.
   B. $248,000.
   C. $312,000.
   D. $318,000.

10. Christine's investment of $3,400,000 in an office building produces the following cash flows:

   Year 1: $2,100,000
   Year 2: $2,200,000
   Year 3: $1,600,000

If the discount rate is 7%, the investment's net present value (NPV) is:

   A. $1,670,749.25.
   B. $1,790,258.62.
   C. $1,920,102.46.
   D. $1,980,638.10.

11. Beta Real Estate Company estimates that an office building, if fully leased, would generate monthly income of $55,000. If a 7% vacancy rate is applied and the capitalization rate is 10%, the current value of the property is:

A. $6,138,000.
B. $6,147,000.
C. $6,290,000.
D. $6,310,000.

12. Cindy owns a 12-year-old house that is worth $339,500. If her house has depreciated at a rate of 2.5% per year, the original value was:

A. $480,000.
B. $485,000.
C. $490,000.
D. $495,000.

13. Leon sold a parcel of land for $484,500 and made a 17% profit on the sale. The purchase price of the land was:

A. $412,846.
B. $413,988.
C. $414,103.
D. $415,092.

14. Delta Real Estate Inc. is considering purchasing an apartment building that is expected to produce annual net income of $68,400. If the company's required rate of return is 9%, the purchase price should be:

A. $740,000.
B. $760,000.
C. $780,000.
D. $800,000.

15. Tony's investment of $200 in a real estate investment trust (REIT) produces the following cash flows:

Year 1: $80
Year 2: $110
Year 3: $120

If the required rate of return is 12%, the investment's net present value (NPV) is:

A. $44.53.
B. $46.18.
C. $48.34.
D. $49.86.

16. If the perpetual rent for a lot is $1,800 per year, and the required rate of return on investment is 8.25%, the value of the lot is:

A. $20,457.54.
B. $20,758.27.
C. $21,818.18.
D. $22,043.29.

17. A subject property has a fifth bedroom that is not present in the comparable, but the comparable has a renovated basement that the subject property does not have. The fifth bedroom is valued at $20,000, and the renovated basement is valued at $15,000. If the comparable recently sold for $560,000, the indicated value of the subject property is:

A. $525,000.
B. $555,000.
C. $565,000.
D. $595,000.

18. Epsilon Real Estate Company provides the following data regarding cash flows for a recent capital project:

Year	0	1	2	3	4	5
Cash flow	–$32,000	$19,000	$6,000	$12,000	$14,000	$3,000

If the company's required rate of return is 6%, the project's net present value (NPV) is:

A. $13,813.96.
B. $14,671.02.
C. $15,092.77.
D. $19,264.65.

19. Mary sold her house for $345,000 and made a 32% profit on the sale. The original purchase price of the house was:

A. $261,364.
B. $262,810.
C. $263,429.
D. $264,812.

20. A comparable house that sold for $315,000 has a finished lower level ($30,000 value) and a third bathroom ($15,000 value) that are not present in the subject. The indicated value of the subject property is:

A. $270,000.
B. $285,000.
C. $310,000.
D. $360,000.

ANSWER KEY

1. B
Step 1: Net operating income = $36,000 - $12,000 = $24,000
Step 2: Property value = $24,000 ÷ 0.14 = $171,428.57

2. D
Step 1: Monthly rental income = $51,600 ÷ 12 months = $4,300
Step 2: Monthly gross rent multiplier = $650,000 ÷ $4,300 = 151.16

3. A
Step 1: Annual net operating income = $3,200 × 12 months = $38,400
Step 2: Capitalization rate = $38,400 ÷ $390,000 = 0.0985 = 9.85%

4. B
Step 1: Year 1 value = $550,000 × 1.04 = $572,000.00
Step 2: Year 2 value = $572,000 × 1.04 = $594,880.00
Step 3: Year 3 value = $594,880 × 1.04 = $618,675.20
Step 4: Time adjustment = $618,675.20 - $550,000 = $68,675.20

5. C
Step 1: Square feet of house = 45 ft. × 55 ft. = 2,475 sq. ft.
Step 2: Original cost of house = 2,475 sq. ft. × $110 per sq. ft. = $272,250
Step 3: Accumulated depreciation = 14 years × 0.025 per year = 0.35
Step 4: Current value of house = $272,250 × (1 - 0.35) = $176,962.50
Step 5: Total property value = $176,962.50 + $95,000 = $271,962.50

6. C
Property value = 85 × $180,000 = $15,300,000

7. D
Step 1: Accumulated depreciation = 6 years × 0.045 per year = 0.27
Step 2: Original value = $255,000 ÷ (1 - 0.27) = $349,315.07

8. D
Step 1: Year 1 value = $195,000 × 1.08 = $210,600.00
Step 2: Year 2 value = $210,600 × 1.08 = $227,448.00
Step 3: Year 3 value = $227,448 × 1.08 = $245,643.84

9. C
Value after storm = $480,000 × (1 - 0.35) = $312,000

10. B
$$NPV = CF_0 + \frac{CF_1}{(1 + r)^1} + \frac{CF_2}{(1 + r)^2} + \frac{CF_3}{(1 + r)^3}$$

$$NPV = -\$3,400,000 + \frac{\$2,100,000}{(1.07)^1} + \frac{\$2,200,000}{(1.07)^2} + \frac{\$1,600,000}{(1.07)^3}$$

$$NPV = -\$3,400,000 + \$1,962,616.82 + \$1,921,565.20 + \$1,306,076.60 = \$1,790,258.62$$

11. A
Step 1: Annual potential gross income = $55,000 × 12 months = $660,000
Step 2: Vacancy allowance = $660,000 × 0.07 = $46,200
Step 3: Net operating income = $660,000 – $46,200 = $613,800
Step 4: Property value = $613,800 ÷ 0.1 = $6,138,000

12. B
Step 1: Accumulated depreciation = 12 years × 0.025 per year = 0.3
Step 2: Original value = $339,500 ÷ (1 – 0.3) = $485,000

13. C
Purchase price = $484,500 ÷ 1.17 = $414,103

14. B
Purchase price = $68,400 ÷ 0.09 = $760,000

15. A

$$NPV = CF_0 + \frac{CF_1}{(1+r)^1} + \frac{CF_2}{(1+r)^2} + \frac{CF_3}{(1+r)^3}$$

$$NPV = -\$200 + \frac{\$80}{(1.12)^1} + \frac{\$110}{(1.12)^2} + \frac{\$120}{(1.12)^3}$$

$$NPV = -\$200 + \$71.43 + \$87.69 + \$85.41 = \$44.53$$

16. C
Value of lot = $1,800 ÷ 0.0825 = $21,818.18

17. C
Value of subject property = $560,000 + $20,000 – $15,000 = $565,000

18. B

$$NPV = CF_0 + \frac{CF_1}{(1+r)^1} + \frac{CF_2}{(1+r)^2} + \frac{CF_3}{(1+r)^3} + \frac{CF_4}{(1+r)^4} + \frac{CF_5}{(1+r)^5}$$

$$NPV = -\$32,000 + \frac{\$19,000}{(1.06)^1} + \frac{\$6,000}{(1.06)^2} + \frac{\$12,000}{(1.06)^3} + \frac{\$14,000}{(1.06)^4} + \frac{\$3,000}{(1.06)^5}$$

$$NPV = -\$32,000 + \$17,924.53 + \$5,339.98 + \$10,075.43 + \$11,089.31 + \$2,241.77 = \$14,671.02$$

19. A
Purchase price = $345,000 ÷ 1.32 = $261,364

20. A
Value of subject property = $315,000 – $30,000 – $15,000 = $270,000

SECTION 5

TAXATION AND ASSESSMENT

QUESTIONS

1. The appraised value of Caleb's house is $2,095,320, and the property tax is based on 23.5% of the appraised value. If the city tax is 45 mills and the county tax is 38 mills, the total annual property tax is:

   A. $33,793.88.
   B. $35,145.52.
   C. $38,472.36.
   D. $40,869.22.

2. A mill is a _____ of a dollar.

   A. tenth
   B. hundredth
   C. thousandth
   D. ten-thousandth

3. Andrea's house was recently appraised for $380,000. If the assessment ratio is 70% and taxes for the year are $6,650, the tax rate is:

   A. 20 mills.
   B. 25 mills.
   C. 30 mills.
   D. 35 mills.

4. Seth's property has a market value of $525,000. If the county's assessment ratio is 75% and the tax rate is 25 mills, the annual property tax is:

   A. $8,875.50.
   B. $9,040.75.
   C. $9,570.25.
   D. $9,843.75.

5. A tax rate of 25 mills is equivalent to _____ for a $100,000 property.

   A. $25
   B. $250
   C. $2,500
   D. $25,000

6. There are _____ mills in one cent.

   A. 10
   B. 100
   C. 1,000
   D. 10,000

7. The maximum exclusion of gain on the sale of a principal residence is _____ for married couples filing a joint tax return, and _____ for single taxpayers.

A. $250,000; $500,000
B. $500,000; $250,000
C. $500,000; $1,000,000
D. $1,000,000; $500,000

8. The Johnsons, a married couple filing a joint tax return, purchased a principal residence in 2015 for $320,000. If they sold the house in 2016 for $390,000, the portion of gain subject to capital gains tax is:

A. $0.
B. $70,000.
C. $250,000.
D. $500,000.

9. Joan's property was recently assessed at $85,300. If the millage rate is 27.5, the annual property tax is:

A. $23.46.
B. $234.58.
C. $2,345.75.
D. $23,457.50.

10. The taxes on Michelle's property are $5,500. If the tax rate is 20 mills and the assessment ratio is 80%, the market value of her property is:

A. $333,750.
B. $338,250.
C. $343,750.
D. $348,250.

11. Jessica's property was recently assessed at $96,000. If the tax rate is $24 per $1,000, the annual property tax is:

A. $2,304.
B. $2,571.
C. $2,779.
D. $2,920.

12. Stephanie purchased a principal residence in 2013 for $700,000. If she sold the house in 2016 for $850,000, the portion of gain subject to capital gains tax is:

A. $0.
B. $25,000.
C. $250,000.
D. $500,000.

13. Ethan's monthly mortgage payment, including principal and interest, is $608.10. If his annual property taxes are $2,370 and his annual homeowner's insurance premium is $366, then his monthly PITI payment is:

   A. $812.20.
   B. $836.10.
   C. $858.90.
   D. $872.40.

14. Susan's property was recently appraised for $450,000. The tax rate is 29.75 mills for the county tax and 22.85 mills for the borough tax. If the rate of assessment is 6%, the total annual property tax is:

   A. $1,369.10.
   B. $1,385.70.
   C. $1,420.20.
   D. $1,468.50.

15. Neal is purchasing a house with a closing date of September 1. If 6 months' taxes of $2,240 were paid in advance on March 1, then Neal will owe the seller:

   A. $0.
   B. $1,120.
   C. $1,680.
   D. $2,240.

16. A millage rate of 54.2 is equivalent to _____ per thousand dollars.

   A. $0.0542
   B. $0.542
   C. $5.42
   D. $54.20

17. Harold purchased a principal residence in 2012 for $175,000. If he sold the house in 2017 for $450,000, the portion of gain subject to capital gains tax is:

   A. $0.
   B. $25,000.
   C. $250,000.
   D. $500,000.

18. If a property has an assessed value of $84,000, and an equalization rate of 1.1 is applied, the equalized value of the property is:

   A. $75,600.
   B. $76,364.
   C. $84,000.
   D. $92,400.

19. Annual property taxes of $1,800 are paid in arrears on January 1 for the previous year. Assuming 30 days per month, if the sale of the property closed on August 15, and the buyer owns the property on the day of closing, the seller will owe the buyer:

A. $680.
B. $750.
C. $1,050.
D. $1,120.

20. The Millers, a married couple filing a joint tax return, purchased a principal residence in 2013 for $450,000. If they sold the house in 2017 for $575,000, the portion of gain subject to capital gains tax is:

A. $0.
B. $125,000.
C. $250,000.
D. $500,000.

21. If the tax rate is 30 mills, the annual tax per dollar of value is:

A. 0.03 cents.
B. 0.3 cents.
C. 3 cents.
D. 30 cents.

22. If a property has an assessed value of $300,000 and an equalized value of $525,000, the equalization rate is:

A. 1.25.
B. 1.50.
C. 1.75.
D. 2.00.

23. Cheryl pays $4,800 in property taxes in advance for the year on January 1. If she sells her house on August 1, the buyer will owe Cheryl:

A. $1,800.
B. $2,000.
C. $2,800.
D. $3,000.

24. Julie's property has a market value of $295,000. It is assessed at 70% of value, less a $10,000 homestead exemption. If the tax rate is 20 mills, the total tax due is:

A. $3,930.
B. $3,990.
C. $4,550.
D. $4,825.

25. Luke pays $1,740 in property taxes for 6 months in advance on March 1. If he sells his house on May 1, the buyer will owe Luke:

    A. $435.
    B. $580.
    C. $1,160.
    D. $1,305.

ANSWER KEY

1. D
Step 1: Assessed value = $2,095,320 × 0.235 = $492,400.20
Step 2: City tax = $492,400.20 × 0.045 = $22,158.01
Step 3: County tax = $492,400.20 × 0.038 = $18,711.21
Step 4: Total property tax = $22,158.01 + $18,711.21 = $40,869.22

2. C
A mill is a thousandth of a dollar.

3. B
Step 1: Assessed value = $380,000 × 0.7 = $266,000
Step 2: Tax rate = $6,650 ÷ $266,000 = 0.025 = 25 mills

4. D
Step 1: Assessed value = $525,000 × 0.75 = $393,750
Step 2: Property tax = $393,750 × 0.025 = $9,843.75

5. C
A tax rate of 25 mills is equivalent to $2,500 for a $100,000 property.

6. A
There are 10 mills in one cent.

7. B
The maximum exclusion of gain on the sale of a principal residence is $500,000 for married couples filing a joint tax return, and $250,000 for single taxpayers.

8. B
Portion of gain subject to capital gains tax = $390,000 – $320,000 = $70,000
The gain on the sale is not excluded because the couple did not own the house and use it as their principal residence during at least 2 of the last 5 years before the date of sale.

9. C
Property tax = $85,300 × 0.0275 = $2,345.75

10. C
Step 1: Assessed value = $5,500 ÷ 0.02 = $275,000
Step 2: Market value = $275,000 ÷ 0.8 = $343,750

11. A
Step 1: Tax rate = $24 ÷ $1,000 = 0.024
Step 2: Property tax = $96,000 × 0.024 = $2,304

12. A
Portion of gain subject to capital gains tax = $0
The maximum exclusion of gain on the sale of a principal residence is $250,000 for single taxpayers who owned the house and used it as a principal residence during at least 2 of the last 5 years before the date of sale.

13. B
Step 1: Monthly property taxes = $2,370 ÷ 12 months = $197.50
Step 2: Monthly insurance premium = $366 ÷ 12 months = $30.50
Step 3: PITI payment = $608.10 + $197.50 + $30.50 = $836.10

14. C
Step 1: Assessed value = $450,000 × 0.06 = $27,000
Step 2: County tax = $27,000 × 0.02975 = $803.25
Step 3: Borough tax = $27,000 × 0.02285 = $616.95
Step 4: Total property tax = $803.25 + $616.95 = $1,420.20

15. A
The buyer takes title to the property on the day the new tax period begins. Therefore, he owes the seller $0.

16. D
A millage rate of 54.2 is equivalent to $54.20 per thousand dollars.

17. B
Step 1: Gain on sale = $450,000 – $175,000 = $275,000
Step 2: Portion of gain subject to capital gains tax = $275,000 – $250,000 = $25,000
The maximum exclusion of gain on the sale of a principal residence is $250,000 for single taxpayers who owned the house and used it as a principal residence during at least 2 of the last 5 years before the date of sale.

18. D
Equalized value = $84,000 × 1.1 = $92,400

19. D
Step 1: Monthly property tax = $1,800 ÷ 12 months = $150
Step 2: Daily property tax = $150 ÷ 30 days = $5
Step 3: The seller owned the property for 7 months and 14 days.
Step 4: Amount seller owes buyer = 7 months × $150 per month = $1,050
Step 5: Amount seller owes buyer = 14 days × $5 per day = $70
Step 6: Total amount seller owes buyer = $1,050 + $70 = $1,120

20. A
Portion of gain subject to capital gains tax = $0
The maximum exclusion of gain on the sale of a principal residence is $500,000 for married couples filing a joint tax return who owned the house and used it as their principal residence during at least 2 of the last 5 years before the date of sale.

21. C
If the tax rate is 30 mills, the annual tax per dollar of value is 3 cents.

22. C
Equalization rate = $525,000 ÷ $300,000 = 1.75

23. B
Step 1: Monthly property tax = $4,800 ÷ 12 months = $400
Step 2: The buyer will own the house for 5 months.
Step 3: Amount buyer owes seller = 5 months × $400 per month = $2,000

24. A
Step 1: Assessed value = $295,000 × 0.7 = $206,500
Step 2: Adjustment for homestead exemption = $206,500 – $10,000 = $196,500
Step 3: Property tax = $196,500 × 0.02 = $3,930

25. C
Step 1: Monthly property tax = $1,740 ÷ 6 months = $290
Step 2: The buyer will own the house for 4 months.
Step 3: Amount buyer owes seller = 4 months × $290 per month = $1,160

SECTION 6

REAL ESTATE INVESTMENT ANALYSIS

QUESTIONS

1. Donald's real estate investment of $205,000 produces gross earnings of 12%. The gross monthly return on Donald's investment is:

   A. $2,050.
   B. $4,100.
   C. $12,300.
   D. $24,600.

2. Sigma Real Estate Corporation purchased an apartment building that currently has 8 vacancies among its 112 units. The vacancy rate is:

   A. 6.98%.
   B. 7.06%.
   C. 7.14%.
   D. 7.30%.

3. Jonathan purchased an investment property for $194,000 and resold it for $226,250. His rate of profit is:

   A. 14.25%.
   B. 16.62%.
   C. 16.98%.
   D. 18.26%.

4. Robin, a property manager, receives a fee of 4% of the first $150,000 of gross rental income received, and 3% of the amount in excess of $150,000. If gross rental income is $245,000, her fee is:

   A. $7,950.
   B. $8,150.
   C. $8,850.
   D. $9,250.

5. Beta Realty Company is considering purchasing an apartment complex for $775,000. If they require a 20% return on investment, the apartment complex should produce annual income of:

   A. $145,000.
   B. $150,000.
   C. $155,000.
   D. $160,000.

6. Arthur purchased a duplex for $460,000 and resold it for $500,000. His gross profit percentage is:

   A. 8.4%.
   B. 8.7%.
   C. 8.9%.
   D. 9.1%.

7. Kristine, a real estate investor, purchased a warehouse for $220,000. If her required rate of return is 13%, the warehouse should produce monthly income of:

   A. $2,186.41.
   B. $2,259.38.
   C. $2,383.33.
   D. $28,600.00.

8. If Jerry sold an investment property for $610,000 and made a 55% return on his investment, then his profit was:

   A. $210,920.
   B. $216,452.
   C. $220,839.
   D. $224,473.

The following information relates to questions 9 – 10.
Christopher, a property manager at an apartment complex, receives compensation equal to 5% of total rent collected. Last month, total rent due was $8,500, but one tenant failed to pay his rent of $900.

9. Based on the information provided, Christopher's compensation received for the month was:

   A. $300.
   B. $330.
   C. $380.
   D. $425.

10. Based on the information provided, Christopher's compensation was _____ lower than it would have been if all the tenants had paid their rent in full.

   A. $45
   B. $90
   C. $450
   D. $900

11. Nancy enters into a contract to rent a house for $1,860 per month. The first month's rent is due before move-in, along with a security deposit equal to three months' rent, plus a pet deposit equal to two months' rent. The total amount that Nancy must pay before moving in to the house is:

    A. $5,580.
    B. $9,300.
    C. $11,160.
    D. $13,020.

12. Mike purchased a building for $1,125,650. If he sells it 6 years later for $1,480,500, the average annual rate of appreciation is:

    A. 5.10%.
    B. 5.25%.
    C. 5.35%.
    D. 5.40%.

The following information relates to questions 13 – 14.
Elizabeth purchased 9 lots for $35,000 each. She kept one-third of the lots for her personal use and sold the remaining lots for a total of $270,000.

13. Based on the information provided, the average sale price of each lot that Elizabeth sold was:

    A. $30,000.
    B. $35,000.
    C. $40,000.
    D. $45,000.

14. Based on the information provided, the rate of profit on each lot sold was:

    A. 27.32%.
    B. 28.57%.
    C. 29.85%.
    D. 30.14%.

15. Colleen rents office space that measures 45 feet by 80 feet. If the monthly rent is $5,200, the annual rent per square foot is:

    A. $1.44.
    B. $1.68.
    C. $17.33.
    D. $17.46.

16. Brian purchased an apartment building for $1,115,000. If his required rate of return is 15%, then he should charge each of his 9 tenants monthly rent of:

    A. $1,309.45.
    B. $1,548.61.
    C. $1,890.25.
    D. $2,143.78.

17. Donna purchased a property for $320,000. If it earns a compounded annual return of 20%, then her property will double in value in:

    A. 1 year.
    B. 2 years.
    C. 3 years.
    D. 4 years.

The following information relates to questions 18 – 20.
Claire sold 3 lots for a total of $100,000. The first lot sold for 2 times the price of the second lot. The second lot sold for 3 times the price of the third lot.

18. Based on the information provided, the first lot sold for:

    A. $10,000.
    B. $30,000.
    C. $40,000.
    D. $60,000.

19. Based on the information provided, the second lot sold for:

    A. $10,000.
    B. $30,000.
    C. $40,000.
    D. $60,000.

20. Based on the information provided, the third lot sold for:

    A. $10,000.
    B. $30,000.
    C. $40,000.
    D. $60,000.

21. Grace owns a property that provides an annual pre-tax cash flow of $18,210. If the initial cash equity is $113,000, the cash-on-cash ratio is:

    A. 13.92%.
    B. 14.76%.
    C. 15.38%.
    D. 16.12%.

22. Larry, a property manager for an apartment building, is permitted to raise rents annu-ally by 4.5% of the cost of improvements made to the property. If apartments currently rent for $975 per month, and Larry spends $8,000 to install a swimming pool, the monthly rent could be raised to:

A. $1,005.
B. $1,008.
C. $1,012.
D. $1,014.

23. Doug would like to purchase a house that costs $476,000. If the land value is 25% of the total price, and the house is 2,650 square feet, the cost per square foot of the house (excluding the land) is:

A. $130.24.
B. $132.56.
C. $134.72.
D. $138.90.

The following information relates to questions 24 – 25.
Delta Management Company can rent out an apartment for $1,100 per month and have the tenant pay utilities, or they can rent out an apartment for $1,500 per month, but the company will pay utilities. Assume that utilities will cost $2,850 per year.

24. Based on the information provided, if the company chose to rent out an apartment for $1,500 and pay for the utilities, the result would be:

A. reduced revenue of $154.50 per month.
B. reduced revenue of $245.50 per month.
C. increased revenue of $162.50 per month.
D. increased revenue of $237.50 per month.

25. Based on the information provided, either rental option is equally viable if utilities cost _____ per year.

A. $3,200
B. $3,600
C. $4,400
D. $4,800

26. Beta Holding Company owns a building that has an effective gross income of $295,000 and a 5% vacancy and collection loss. If debt services are $18,000 and allowable ex-penses are $92,000, the net operating income is:

A. $188,250.
B. $203,000.
C. $221,000.
D. $235,750.

27. If a property's economic life is 27.5 years, the property depreciates _____ each year.

    A. 3.46%
    B. 3.64%
    C. 4.36%
    D. 4.63%

28. Terry sold a property for $1,708,000, which was 140% of what she paid for it 5 years earlier. The original purchase price of Terry's property was:

    A. $1,220,000.
    B. $1,280,000.
    C. $1,340,000.
    D. $1,390,000.

29. If an apartment building depreciates 2% per year, its economic life is:

    A. 10 years.
    B. 20 years.
    C. 25 years.
    D. 50 years.

The following information relates to questions 30 – 32.
Alpha Development Company is considering purchasing a building with 60,000 leasable square feet. The company estimates that they can rent to tenants for $16 per square foot, and the vacancy rate will be 8%. They also expect to generate $3,500 each year in additional miscellaneous income.

30. Based on the information provided, the potential gross income is:

    A. $956,500.
    B. $960,000.
    C. $973,500.
    D. $980,000.

31. Based on the information provided, the vacancy allowance is:

    A. $76,520.
    B. $76,440.
    C. $76,800.
    D. $78,400.

32. Based on the information provided, the effective gross income is:

    A. $886,700.
    B. $908,400.
    C. $924,300.
    D. $963,500.

33. Beta Properties Inc. purchased a lot for $300,000 and then improved it by building a duplex valued at $1,200,000. The improvement ratio is:

A. 1:3.
B. 1:4.
C. 3:1.
D. 4:1.

34. Laura purchased a duplex for $620,000. If it has a 20-year life, then it will be worth $372,000 in:

A. 7 years.
B. 8 years.
C. 9 years.
D. 10 years.

35. Matt purchased a house for $413,000. If the purchase price was 70% of what he sold it for 8 years later, the selling price was:

A. $289,100.
B. $536,900.
C. $590,000.
D. $702,100.

36. Delta Retail Company entered into a rental agreement that requires them to pay rent of $850 per month plus 3.25% of gross annual sales exceeding $75,000. If the company's gross annual sales were $110,000 last year, the average monthly rent was:

A. $929.07.
B. $936.12.
C. $940.23.
D. $944.79.

The following information relates to questions 37 – 39.
Tracey, the property manager of an apartment building, provides the following annual data to a potential investor regarding the subject property:

Potential gross income	$95,000
Miscellaneous income	$2,000
Debt services	$23,000
Administrative expenses	$800
Vacancy and collection allowance	$15,000
Maintenance expenses	$1,000
Utilities	$8,000

37. Based on the information provided, the effective gross income is:

    A. $68,500.
    B. $72,200.
    C. $82,000.
    D. $84,800.

38. Based on the information provided, the net operating income is:

    A. $72,200.
    B. $76,400.
    C. $82,000.
    D. $83,960.

39. Based on the information provided, the before-tax cash flow is:

    A. $46,920.
    B. $49,200.
    C. $57,010.
    D. $60,200.

40. Francis, a real estate developer, must purchase an insurance policy to protect against potential losses at his job site. If a $500,000 insurance policy has a cost of $0.55 per $100, the annual premium is:

    A. $2,750.
    B. $3,000.
    C. $3,250.
    D. $3,500.

41. If a building has a 25-year economic life, it will depreciate _____ per year.

    A. 2%
    B. 3%
    C. 4%
    D. 5%

42. Lindsay is purchasing a condo with a closing date of April 18. The homeowners' association fee of $360 is due at the beginning of each month. If Lindsay is charged for the day of closing, she will owe the seller:

    A. $147.
    B. $156.
    C. $163.
    D. $178.

43. Nathan purchased a building for $410,000. If it has a total useful life of 25 years, then its value after 7 years is:

   A. $293,600.
   B. $295,200.
   C. $302,700.
   D. $304,300.

44. If an apartment building depreciates 3.5% per year, then it will be worth 30% of its original value in:

   A. 9 years.
   B. 12 years.
   C. 17 years.
   D. 20 years.

45. Sigma Development Corporation owns a building valued at $240,000 that has an economic life of 15 years. If the building's effective age is 3 years, and the lot is valued at $30,000, then the total value of the property is:

   A. $218,000.
   B. $220,000.
   C. $222,000.
   D. $224,000.

46. Raj owns a building that has potential gross income of $350,000 and a vacancy rate of 5%. If the building produces miscellaneous income of $14,000, the effective gross income is:

   A. $346,500.
   B. $354,500.
   C. $364,000.
   D. $381,500.

47. Tim is a real estate investor with a required annual return of 12%. If he owns a property valued at $420,000, then it should produce monthly income of:

   A. $3,800.
   B. $4,200.
   C. $48,200.
   D. $50,400.

48. Joe purchased a building for $980,000. If it has a useful life of 25 years, then it will be worth $705,600 in:

   A. 6 years.
   B. 7 years.
   C. 8 years.
   D. 9 years.

The following information relates to questions 49 – 50.
Jason owns an apartment complex with 8 units. Currently 4 units rent for $1,250 per month, 3 units rent for $480 per week, and the last unit is vacant. The semiannual property expenses are $7,300.

49. Based on the information provided, the net operating income is:

   A. $118,560.
   B. $119,810.
   C. $120,280.
   D. $121,960.

50. Based on the information provided, the vacancy rate is:

   A. 6.5%.
   B. 8.5%.
   C. 9.5%.
   D. 12.5%.

51. Jeff purchased an investment property 3 years ago for $290,000. He made improvements of $27,000 and claimed $34,800 in depreciation. If he sells the property for $380,000, his capital gain is:

   A. $82,200.
   B. $90,000.
   C. $97,800.
   D. $151,800.

52. Bridgette is interested in purchasing an apartment building that earns gross annual rent of $32,000. A comparable property recently sold for $420,000 that earned gross annual rent of $52,500. Using the rent multiplier method, the value of the apartment building that Bridgette is considering is:

   A. $256,000.
   B. $264,000.
   C. $272,000.
   D. $280,000.

53. Lisa is selling an apartment that is scheduled to close on November 12. She collected rent for November on the first of the month in the amount of $1,200. If the buyer is due the rental income for the day of closing, Lisa will owe the buyer:

   A. $740.
   B. $760.
   C. $780.
   D. $800.

The following information relates to questions 54 – 55.
Beth owns a building valued at $605,000. Over a 10-year period, the building has depreciated to $363,000.

54. Based on the information provided, the building depreciates _____ per year.

   A. 3%
   B. 4%
   C. 5%
   D. 6%

55. Based on the information provided, the building's useful life is:

   A. 15 years.
   B. 20 years.
   C. 25 years.
   D. 35 years.

ANSWER KEY

1. A
Step 1: Annual return = $205,000 × 0.12 = $24,600
Step 2: Monthly return = $24,600 ÷ 12 months = $2,050 per month

2. C
Vacancy rate = 8 vacancies ÷ 112 units = 0.0714 = 7.14%

3. B
Rate of profit = ($226,250 – $194,000) ÷ $194,000 = 0.1662 = 16.62%

4. C
Step 1: Fee on the first $150,000 = $150,000 × 0.04 = $6,000
Step 2: Fee on amount over $150,000 = ($245,000 – $150,000) × 0.03 = $2,850
Step 3: Total fee = $6,000 + $2,850 = $8,850

5. C
Annual income = $775,000 × 0.2 = $155,000

6. B
Gross profit percentage = ($500,000 – $460,000) ÷ $460,000 = 0.087 = 8.7%

7. C
Step 1: Annual income = $220,000 × 0.13 = $28,600
Step 2: Monthly income = $28,600 ÷ 12 months = $2,383.33 per month

8. B
Step 1: Purchase price = $610,000 ÷ 1.55 = $393,548
Step 2: Profit = $610,000 – $393,548 = $216,452

9. C
Step 1: Rent collected = $8,500 – $900 = $7,600
Step 2: Compensation = $7,600 × 0.05 = $380

10. A
Reduced compensation = $900 × 0.05 = $45

11. C
Step 1: Security deposit = $1,860 × 3 = $5,580
Step 2: Pet deposit = $1,860 × 2 = $3,720
Step 3: Total amount payable = $1,860 + $5,580 + $3,720 = $11,160

12. B
Step 1: Total profit = ($1,480,500 – $1,125,650) ÷ $1,125,650 = 0.3152
Step 2: Annual rate of appreciation = 0.3152 ÷ 6 years = 0.0525 = 5.25% per year

13. D
Step 1: Lots sold = 9 lots × 2/3 = 6 lots
Step 2: Average sale price = $270,000 ÷ 6 lots = $45,000 per lot

14. B
Rate of profit = ($45,000 – $35,000) ÷ $35,000 = 0.2857 = 28.57%

15. C
Step 1: Annual rent = $5,200 × 12 months = $62,400
Step 2: Area of office space = 45 ft. × 80 ft. = 3,600 sq. ft.
Step 3: Annual rent per square foot = $62,400 ÷ 3,600 sq. ft. = $17.33 per sq. ft.

16. B
Step 1: Annual income = $1,115,000 × 0.15 = $167,250
Step 2: Monthly income = $167,250 ÷ 12 months = $13,937.50
Step 3: Monthly rent per tenant = $13,937.50 ÷ 9 tenants = $1,548.61 per tenant

17. D
Year 1 value = $320,000 × 1.2 = $384,000
Year 2 value = $384,000 × 1.2 = $460,800
Year 3 value = $460,800 × 1.2 = $552,960
Year 4 value = $552,960 × 1.2 = $663,552

18. D
Step 1: Let the third lot = Y, let the second lot = 3 × Y, let the first lot = 2 × 3 × Y
Step 2: Y + (3 × Y) + (2 × 3 × Y) = 10Y = $100,000; therefore Y = $10,000
Step 3: Selling price of first lot = 2 × 3 × Y = 2 × 3 × $10,000 = $60,000

19. B
Step 1: Let the third lot = Y, let the second lot = 3 × Y, let the first lot = 2 × 3 × Y
Step 2: Y + (3 × Y) + (2 × 3 × Y) = 10Y = $100,000; therefore Y = $10,000
Step 3: Selling price of second lot = 3 × Y = 3 × $10,000 = $30,000

20. A
Step 1: Let the third lot = Y, let the second lot = 3 × Y, let the first lot = 2 × 3 × Y
Step 2: Y + (3 × Y) + (2 × 3 × Y) = 10Y = $100,000; therefore Y = $10,000
Step 3: Selling price of third lot = Y = $10,000

21. D
Cash-on-cash ratio = $18,210 ÷ $113,000 = 0.1612 = 16.12%

22. A
Step 1: Annual rent increase = $8,000 × 0.045 = $360
Step 2: Monthly rent increase = $360 ÷ 12 months = $30 per month
Step 3: New monthly rent= $975 + $30 = $1,005

23. C
Step 1: Value of house = $476,000 × (1 – 0.25) = $357,000
Step 2: Cost per square foot = $357,000 ÷ 2,650 sq. ft. = $134.72 per sq. ft.

24. C
Step 1: Monthly utilities = $2,850 ÷ 12 months = $237.50 per month
Step 2: Difference in rent attributed to utilities = $1,500 – $1,100 = $400 per month
Step 3: Increased monthly revenue = $400 – $237.50 = $162.50

25. D
Step 1: Difference in rent attributed to utilities = $1,500 – $1,100 = $400
Step 2: Utilities breakeven = $400 × 12 months = $4,800

26. B
Formula: Net operating income = Effective gross income – Allowable expenses
Net operating income = $295,000 – $92,000 = $203,000

27. B
Annual depreciation = 1 ÷ 27.5 years = 0.0364 = 3.64% per year

28. A
Original purchase price = $1,708,000 ÷ 1.4 = $1,220,000

29. D
Economic life = 100% ÷ 2% per year = 50 years

30. B
Potential gross income = $16 per sq. ft. × 60,000 sq. ft. = $960,000

31. C
Step 1: Potential gross income = $16 per sq. ft. × 60,000 sq. ft. = $960,000
Step 2: Vacancy allowance = $960,000 × 0.08 = $76,800

32. A
Formula: Effective gross income = Potential gross income – Vacancy and collection allowance + Miscellaneous income
Effective gross income = $960,000 – $76,800 + $3,500 = $886,700

33. D
Improvement ratio = $1,200,000 ÷ $300,000 = 4:1

34. B
Step 1: Annual depreciation = 1 ÷ 20 years = 0.05 per year
Step 2: Accumulated depreciation = 1 – ($372,000 ÷ $620,000) = 0.4
Step 3: Number of years = 0.4 ÷ 0.05 per year = 8 years

35. C
Selling price = $413,000 ÷ 0.7 = $590,000

36. D
Step 1: Annual rent based on sales = ($110,000 – $75,000) × 0.0325 = $1,137.50
Step 2: Monthly rent based on sales = $1,137.50 ÷ 12 months = $94.79 per month
Step 3: Average monthly rent = $850 + $94.79 = $944.79

37. C
Formula: Effective gross income = Potential gross income – Vacancy and collection allowance + Miscellaneous income
Effective gross income = $95,000 – $15,000 + $2,000 = $82,000

38. A
Formula: Net operating income = Effective gross income − Maintenance expenses − Administrative expenses − Utilities
Net operating income = $82,000 − $1,000 − $800 − $8,000 = $72,200

39. B
Before-tax cash flow = Net operating income − Debt services
Before-tax cash flow = $72,200 − $23,000 = $49,200

40. A
Step 1: Premium rate = $0.55 ÷ $100 = 0.0055
Step 2: Annual premium = $500,000 × 0.0055 = $2,750

41. C
Annual depreciation = 1 ÷ 25 years = 0.04 = 4% per year

42. B
Step 1: Daily homeowners' association fee = $360 ÷ 30 days = $12 per day
Step 2: The buyer will own the property for 13 days.
Step 3: Amount buyer owes seller = 13 days × $12 per day = $156

43. B
Step 1: Annual deprecation = 1 ÷ 25 years = 0.04 per year
Step 2: Accumulated depreciation = 7 years × 0.04 = 0.28
Step 3: Value after 7 years = $410,000 × (1 − 0.28) = $295,200

44. D
Number of years = (1 − 0.3) ÷ 0.035 per year = 20 years

45. C
Step 1: Annual depreciation = $240,000 ÷ 15 years = $16,000
Step 2: Accumulated depreciation = $16,000 per year × 3 years = $48,000
Step 3: Total value of property = $240,000 − $48,000 + $30,000 = $222,000

46. A
Formula: Effective gross income = Potential gross income − Vacancy and collection allowance + Miscellaneous income
Effective gross income = $350,000 − ($350,000 × 0.05) + $14,000 = $346,500

47. B
Step 1: Annual income = $420,000 × 0.12 = $50,400
Step 2: Monthly income = $50,400 ÷ 12 months = $4,200 per month

48. B
Step 1: Annual depreciation = 1 ÷ 25 years = 0.04 per year
Step 2: Accumulated depreciation = 1 − ($705,600 ÷ $980,000) = 0.28
Step 3: Number of years = 0.28 ÷ 0.04 per year = 7 years

49. C
Step 1: Monthly rent in annual terms = 4 units × $1,250 per unit × 12 months = $60,000
Step 2: Weekly rent in annual terms = 3 units × $480 per unit × 52 weeks = $74,880
Step 3: Semiannual expenses in annual terms = $7,300 × 2 periods = $14,600
Step 4: Net operating income = $60,000 + $74,880 – $14,600 = $120,280

50. D
Vacancy rate = 1 vacancy ÷ 8 units = 0.125 = 12.5%

51. C
Step 1: Total investment = $290,000 + $27,000 – $34,800 = $282,200
Step 2: Capital gain = $380,000 – $282,200 = $97,800

52. A
Step 1: Gross rent multiplier = $420,000 ÷ $52,500 = 8
Step 2: Value of property = $32,000 × 8 = $256,000

53. B
Step 1: Daily rent = $1,200 ÷ 30 days = $40 per day
Step 2: The buyer will own the property for 19 days.
Step 3: Amount seller owes buyer = 19 days × $40 per day = $760

54. B
Step 1: Accumulated depreciation = 1 – ($363,000 ÷ $605,000) = 0.4
Step 2: Annual depreciation = 0.4 ÷ 10 years = 0.04 = 4% per year

55. C
Step 1: Accumulated depreciation = 1 – ($363,000 ÷ $605,000) = 0.4
Step 2: Annual depreciation = 0.4 ÷ 10 years = 0.04 per year
Step 3: Useful life = 1 ÷ 0.04 per year = 25 years

SECTION 7

FUNDAMENTAL MATH CONCEPTS

QUESTIONS

1. Frank deposited $150 in an interest-bearing account earning 6% annually. Assuming the interest is not withdrawn, the amount of interest earned in the third year will be:

   A. $9.00.
   B. $9.54.
   C. $10.11.
   D. $10.72.

2. Housing prices have varied by the following amounts over the past 7 years: –3%, +4%, +5%, –3%, +2%, +6%, –1%. The mean, median, and mode of the data, respectively, is:

   A. 1.43%; –3%; 2%.
   B. 1.43%; 2%; –3%.
   C. 2.86%; –3%; 2%.
   D. 2.86%; 2%; –3%.

3. The reciprocal of 8 can be expressed as:

   A. 0.125.
   B. 0.156.
   C. 0.250.
   D. 0.256.

4. If a real estate investor sold 55 houses this year and 47 houses last year, the percent fewer houses sold last year was:

   A. 15.08%.
   B. 16.13%.
   C. 17.02%.
   D. 18.11%.

5. If $1 is deposited in an interest-bearing account earning 8.5% annually, and the interest is not withdrawn, the account value at the end of 25 years will be:

   A. $7.44.
   B. $7.69.
   C. $8.02.
   D. $8.13.

6. If $1 is deposited each year in an interest-bearing account earning 8.5% annually, and the interest is not withdrawn, the account value at the end of 25 years will be:

   A. $70.04.
   B. $72.89.
   C. $74.12.
   D. $78.67.

7. The present value of $1 earning 7% interest annually for 6 years is:

    A. $0.62.
    B. $0.67.
    C. $0.72.
    D. $0.77.

8. An annual interest rate of 4.7% is equivalent to:

    A. 0.392% monthly or 1.175% quarterly.
    B. 0.392% monthly or 1.573% quarterly.
    C. 1.175% quarterly or 0.412% monthly.
    D. 2.352% quarterly or 0.783% monthly.

9. A monthly interest rate of 0.9% is equivalent to:

    A. 1.8% quarterly or 5.4% annually.
    B. 2.7% quarterly or 8.1% annually.
    C. 2.7% quarterly or 10.8% annually.
    D. 5.4% quarterly or 10.8% annually.

10. A quarterly interest rate of 3.2% is equivalent to:

    A. 1.07% monthly or 9.60% annually.
    B. 1.07% monthly or 12.80% annually.
    C. 6.40% monthly or 9.60% annually.
    D. 6.40% monthly or 12.80% annually.

11. Ruth owns an investment yielding an 18% pre-tax return. If she is in the 28% tax bracket, the equivalent after-tax return is:

    A. 5.04%.
    B. 12.96%.
    C. 14.28%.
    D. 23.04%.

12. Beta Corporation purchased an office building and will rent out 5 floors that each measure 46,000 square feet. On each floor, 20% of the square footage must be set aside for hallways and common areas. If each office needs to be at least 1,600 square feet, Beta Corporation can rent a total of:

    A. 115 offices.
    B. 116 offices.
    C. 128 offices.
    D. 129 offices.

13. The formula for the area of a triangle is:

    A. ½ Base × Height.
    B. ½ Base × ½ Height.
    C. ½ Base × Height^2.
    D. Base^2 × ½ Height.

14. A crew is hired to paint a large triangular portion of a building's interior. If the width of the section is 56 feet and the height is 23 feet, the crew will need to paint:

    A. 322 square feet.
    B. 483 square feet.
    C. 644 square feet.
    D. 805 square feet.

15. The formula for the area of a circle is:

    A. $\pi \times r^2$.
    B. $\pi \times D^2$.
    C. $\pi^2 \times r^2$.
    D. $\pi \times D$.

16. Kathy is installing a circular swimming pool that is 18 feet in diameter. The area of the swimming pool is:

    A. 56.55 square feet.
    B. 254.47 square feet.
    C. 316.24 square feet.
    D. 1,017.88 square feet.

17. The formula for the volume of a triangular-shaped object is:

    A. ½ Base × ½ Height × Length.
    B. ½ Base × ½ Height × ½ Length.
    C. ½ Base × Height × Length.
    D. Base × Height × Length.

18. Gary's house has a triangular-shaped attic that needs to be heated throughout the winter. If the dimensions of the attic are 32 feet by 12 feet by 56 feet, the volume of space that needs to be heated is:

    A. 10,408 cubic feet.
    B. 10,515 cubic feet.
    C. 10,646 cubic feet.
    D. 10,752 cubic feet.

19. The formula for the volume of a cylindrical-shaped object is:

    A. $\pi \times D \times$ Height.
    B. $\pi \times r^2 \times$ Height.
    C. $\pi \times r^2 \times \frac{1}{2}$ Height.
    D. $\pi \times r \times$ Height.

20. A farmer is installing a silo that is 22 feet in diameter and 42 feet high. The volume of the silo is:

    A. 2,902.8 cubic feet.
    B. 7,982.8 cubic feet.
    C. 15,965.6 cubic feet.
    D. 16,257.4 cubic feet.

21. 19.5 feet + 18.6 inches + 14.4 yards = ____

    A. 61.70 feet
    B. 62.85 feet
    C. 63.90 feet
    D. 64.25 feet

22. A rectangular container measuring 3.75 feet by 4.6 yards by 10.2 inches contains:

    A. 43.07 cubic feet.
    B. 43.99 cubic feet.
    C. 44.13 cubic feet.
    D. 44.57 cubic feet.

The following information relates to questions 23 – 25.
Michael wants to install a tennis court on his property that measures 78 feet by 9 yards, and is 6 inches thick. The cost of concrete is estimated to be $90 per cubic yard.

23. Based on the information provided, the volume of cubic feet of concrete needed to complete the project is:

    A. 1,053.
    B. 1,124.
    C. 1,360.
    D. 4,212.

24. Based on the information provided, the volume of cubic yards of concrete needed to complete the project is:

    A. 37.
    B. 39.
    C. 41.
    D. 43.

25. Based on the information provided, the cost of the concrete needed to complete the project is:

  A. $3,305.
  B. $3,470.
  C. $3,510.
  D. $3,680.

26. Madeline owns a warehouse that she will rent out for $0.85 per cubic foot per year. If the dimensions of the warehouse are 11 yards by 32 yards by 18 feet high, the monthly rent will be:

  A. $3,294.50.
  B. $4,039.20.
  C. $12,117.60.
  D. $48,470.40.

The following information relates to questions 27 – 29.
Lawrence would like to build a 5-foot high fence around his front yard. His house is 60 feet wide, and the dimensions of his front yard are 120 feet by 90 feet. The materials needed to build the fence are $4.10 per square yard and the labor cost is $1.60 per square yard. Lawrence estimates that each year the cost to maintain the fence will be $0.90 per square yard.

27. Based on the information provided, the cost of materials needed to build the fence is:

  A. $760.
  B. $780.
  C. $800.
  D. $820.

28. Based on the information provided, the cost of labor to install the fence is:

  A. $300.
  B. $320.
  C. $340.
  D. $360.

29. Based on the information provided, the total cost to build the fence and maintain it for the first year is:

  A. $1,280.
  B. $1,300.
  C. $1,320.
  D. $1,340.

30. Taylor would like to carpet a room that measures 12 feet by 15 feet. If the price of carpet is $29 per square yard, the total cost will be:

A. $580.
B. $870.
C. $1,740.
D. $5,220.

The following information relates to questions 31 – 34.

Jordan would like to repave his driveway that is 18 feet wide, 50 feet long, and 6 inches thick. Concrete costs $95 per cubic yard and labor costs $3.30 per square foot.

31. Based on the information provided, the volume of concrete needed to repave the driveway is:

A. 400 cubic feet.
B. 425 cubic feet.
C. 450 cubic feet.
D. 475 cubic feet.

32. Based on the information provided, the cost of concrete needed to repave the driveway is:

A. $1,438.85.
B. $1,583.65.
C. $1,610.25.
D. $1,732.55.

33. Based on the information provided, the cost of labor to repave the driveway is:

A. $2,910.
B. $2,930.
C. $2,950.
D. $2,970.

34. Based on the information provided, Jordan's total cost is:

A. $4,382.85.
B. $4,553.65.
C. $4,792.55.
D. $4,937.35.

35. Josh owns an investment yielding an after-tax return of 9.5%. If he is in the 15% tax bracket, the equivalent pre-tax return is:

A. 1.43%.
B. 8.08%.
C. 10.93%.
D. 11.18%.

36. A local municipality is planning to repave neighborhood streets at a cost of $36 per foot of frontage. The municipality will pay for 40% of the cost and the homeowners must pay the remaining balance. If Roger's lot has frontage of 115 feet, and there is an identical lot directly across the street, then Roger must pay:

    A. $1,242.
    B. $1,268.
    C. $2,480.
    D. $2,496.

37. Pauline, a retail store owner, must pay annual rent of $32.50 per square foot in addition to 4.75% of annual gross sales exceeding $150,000. If the dimensions of the store are 50 feet by 110 feet, and $625,000 of merchandise is sold during the year, the annual rent will be:

    A. $195,320.85.
    B. $198,725.60.
    C. $201,312.50.
    D. $204,580.25.

The following information relates to questions 38 – 40.
Nora's income is $80,000 and she is in the 25% tax bracket. While preparing to file her tax return, she expected to take an $8,000 deduction through a government incentive program that she qualified for. However, she has discovered the deduction has been replaced with a $4,000 tax credit.

38. Ignoring exemptions and other adjustments, if Nora had claimed the $8,000 tax deduction, her total taxes owed would have been:

    A. $14,000.
    B. $16,000.
    C. $18,000.
    D. $20,000.

39. Ignoring exemptions and other adjustments, if Nora claims the $4,000 tax credit, her total taxes owed will be:

    A. $14,000.
    B. $16,000.
    C. $18,000.
    D. $20,000.

40. Ignoring exemptions and other adjustments, a tax credit of _____ would result in the same amount of taxes owed as the $8,000 tax deduction.

    A. $2,000
    B. $3,000
    C. $5,000
    D. $6,000

ANSWER KEY

1. C
Step 1: Year 1 value = $150.00 \times 1.06 = \$159.00$
Step 2: Year 2 value = $159.00 \times 1.06 = \$168.54$
Step 3: Year 3 value = $168.54 \times 1.06 = \$178.65$
Step 4: Interest earned in third year = $\$178.65 - \$168.54 = \$10.11$

2. B
Mean = $[(-3\%)+(4\%)+(5\%)+(-3\%)+(2\%)+(6\%)+(-1\%)] \div 7 = 1.43\%$
Median = $-3\%, -3\%, -1\%, \underline{+2\%}, +4\%, +5\%, +6\% = 2\%$
Mode = -3% is the only number that appears twice, therefore it is the mode.

3. A
The reciprocal of 8 can be expressed as 1/8 or 0.125.

4. C
Percent change = (55 houses – 47 houses) ÷ 47 houses = 0.1702 = 17.02%

5. B
$S^n = (1 + i)^n$
$S^n = (1.085)^{25} = \$7.69$

6. D
$S_n = [(1 + i)^n - 1] \div i$
$S_n = [(1.085)^{25} - 1] \div 0.085 = \$78.67$

7. B
$V^n = 1 \div [(1 + i)^n]$
$V^n = 1 \div [(1.07)^6] = \$0.67$

8. A
Monthly interest rate = 4.7% ÷ 12 months = 0.392%
Quarterly interest rate = 4.7% ÷ 4 quarters = 1.175%

9. C
Quarterly interest rate = 0.9% × 3 months = 2.7%
Annual interest rate = 0.9% × 12 months = 10.8%

10. B
Monthly interest rate = 3.2% ÷ 3 months = 1.07%
Annual interest rate = 3.2% × 4 quarters = 12.80%

11. B
After-tax return = 0.18 × (1 – 0.28) = 12.96%

12. A
Step 1: Area for hallways and common areas = 46,000 sq. ft. × 0.2 = 9,200 sq. ft.
Step 2: Remaining area for offices = 46,000 sq. ft. – 9,200 sq. ft. = 36,800 sq. ft.
Step 3: Number of offices per floor = 36,800 sq. ft. ÷ 1,600 sq. ft. per office = 23 offices
Step 4: Total number of offices = 23 offices per floor × 5 floors = 115 offices

13. A
Area of a triangle = ½ Base × Height

14. C
Area = ½ Base × Height
Area = 0.5 × 56 ft. × 23 ft. = 644 sq. ft.

15. A
Area of a circle = $\pi \times r^2$

16. B
Area = $\pi \times r^2$
Area = 3.1416 × 9 ft.^{2} = 254.47 sq. ft.

17. C
Volume of a triangular-shaped object = ½ Base × Height × Length

18. D
Volume = ½ Base × Height × Length
Volume = 0.5 × 32 ft. × 12 ft. × 56 ft. = 10,752 cu. ft.

19. B
Volume of a cylindrical-shaped object = $\pi \times r^2 \times$ Height

20. C
Volume = $\pi \times r^2 \times$ Height
Volume = 3.1416 × 11 ft.^{2} × 42 ft. = 15,965.6 cu. ft.

21. D
Step 1: Convert inches to feet = 18.6 in. ÷ 12 in. per ft. = 1.55 ft.
Step 2: Convert yards to feet = 14.4 yd. × 3 ft. per yd. = 43.2 ft.
Step 3: Total length = 19.5 ft. + 1.55 ft. + 43.2 ft. = 64.25 ft.

22. B
Step 1: Convert yards to feet = 4.6 yd. × 3 ft. per yd. = 13.8 ft.
Step 2: Convert inches to feet = 10.2 in. ÷ 12 in. per ft. = 0.85 ft.
Step 3: Volume = 3.75 ft. × 13.8 ft. × 0.85 ft. = 43.99 cu. ft.

23. A
Step 1: Convert yards to feet = 9 yd. × 3 ft. per yd. = 27 ft.
Step 2: Convert inches to feet = 6 in. ÷ 12 in. per ft. = 0.5 ft.
Step 3: Volume = 78 ft. × 27 ft. × 0.5 ft. = 1,053 cu. ft.

24. B
Conversion factor: 1 cu. yd. = 27 cu. ft.
Step 1: Convert yards to feet = 9 yd. × 3 ft. per yd. = 27 ft.
Step 2: Convert inches to feet = 6 in. ÷ 12 in. per ft. = 0.5 ft.
Step 3: Volume in cubic feet = 78 ft. × 27 ft. × 0.5 ft. = 1,053 cu. ft.
Step 4: Volume in cubic yards = 1,053 cu. ft. ÷ 27 cu. ft. per cu. yd. = 39 cu. yd.

25. C
Conversion factor: 1 cu. yd. = 27 cu. ft.
Step 1: Convert yards to feet = 9 yd. × 3 ft. per yd. = 27 ft.
Step 2: Convert inches to feet = 6 in. ÷ 12 in. per ft. = 0.5 ft.
Step 3: Volume in cubic feet = 78 ft. × 27 ft. × 0.5 ft. = 1,053 cu. ft.
Step 4: Volume in cubic yards = 1,053 cu. ft. ÷ 27 cu. ft. per cu. yd. = 39 cu. yd.
Step 5: Total cost = 39 cu. yd. × $90 per cu. yd. = $3,510

26. B
Step 1: Convert yards to feet = 11 yd. × 3 ft. per yd. = 33 ft.
Step 2: Convert yards to feet = 32 yd. × 3 ft. per yd. = 96 ft.
Step 3: Volume = 33 ft. × 96 ft. × 18 ft. = 57,024 cu. ft.
Step 4: Annual rent = 57,024 cu. ft. × $0.85 per cu. ft. = $48,470.40
Step 5: Monthly rent = $48,470.40 ÷ 12 months = $4,039.20 per month

27. D
Conversion factor: 1 sq. yd. = 9 sq. ft.
Step 1: Perimeter of yard to be fenced = 120 ft. + 90 ft. + 120 ft. + 90 ft. – 60 ft. = 360 ft.
Step 2: Amount of materials needed = 360 ft. × 5 ft. = 1,800 sq. ft.
Step 3: Convert to square yards = 1,800 sq. ft. ÷ 9 sq. ft. per sq. yd. = 200 sq. yd.
Step 4: Cost of materials = 200 sq. yd. × $4.10 per sq. yd. = $820

28. B
Conversion factor: 1 sq. yd. = 9 sq. ft.
Step 1: Perimeter of yard to be fenced = 120 ft. + 90 ft. + 120 ft. + 90 ft. – 60 ft. = 360 ft.
Step 2: Amount of materials needed = 360 ft. × 5 ft. = 1,800 sq. ft.
Step 3: Convert to square yards = 1,800 sq. ft. ÷ 9 sq. ft. per sq. yd. = 200 sq. yd.
Step 4: Cost of labor = 200 sq. yd. × $1.60 per sq. yd. = $320.00

29. C
Conversion factor: 1 sq. yd. = 9 sq. ft.
Step 1: Perimeter of yard to be fenced = 120 ft. + 90 ft. + 120 ft. + 90 ft. – 60 ft. = 360 ft.
Step 2: Amount of materials needed = 360 ft. × 5 ft. = 1,800 sq. ft.
Step 3: Convert to square yards = 1,800 sq. ft. ÷ 9 sq. ft. per sq. yd. = 200 sq. yd.
Step 4: Total cost = 200 sq. yd. × ($4.10 + $1.60 + $0.90 per sq. yd.) = $1,320

30. A
Conversion factor: 1 sq. yd. = 9 sq. ft.
Step 1: Area = 12 ft. × 15 ft. = 180 sq. ft.
Step 2: Convert to square yards = 180 sq. ft. ÷ 9 sq. ft. per sq. yd. = 20 sq. yd.
Step 3: Total cost = 20 sq. yd. × $29 per sq. yd. = $580

31. C
Step 1: Convert inches to feet = 6 in. ÷ 12 in. per ft. = 0.5 ft.
Step 2: Volume = 18 ft. × 50 ft. × 0.5 ft. = 450 cu. ft.

32. B
Conversion factor: 1 cu. yd. = 27 cu. ft.
Step 1: Convert inches to feet = 6 in. ÷ 12 in. per ft. = 0.5 ft.
Step 2: Volume in cubic feet = 18 ft. × 50 ft. × 0.5 ft. = 450 cu. ft.
Step 3: Volume in cubic yards = 450 cu. ft. ÷ 27 cu. ft. per cu. yd. = 16.67 cu. yd.
Step 4: Cost of concrete = 16.67 cu. yd. × $95 per cu. yd. = $1,583.65

33. D
Step 1: Area = 18 ft. × 50 ft. = 900 sq. ft.
Step 2: Cost of labor = 900 sq. ft. × $3.30 per sq. ft. = $2,970

34. B
Conversion factor: 1 cu. yd. = 27 cu. ft.
Step 1: Convert inches to feet = 6 in. ÷ 12 in. per ft. = 0.5 ft.
Step 2: Volume in cubic feet = 18 ft. × 50 ft. × 0.5 ft. = 450 cu. ft.
Step 3: Volume in cubic yards = 450 cu. ft. ÷ 27 cu. ft. per cu. yd. = 16.67 cu. yd.
Step 4: Cost of concrete = 16.67 cu. yd. × $95 per cu. yd. = $1,583.65
Step 5: Area = 18 ft. × 50 ft. = 900 sq. ft.
Step 6: Cost of labor = 900 sq. ft. × $3.30 per sq. ft. = $2,970
Step 7: Total cost = $1,583.65 + $2,970 = $4,553.65

35. D
Pre-tax return = 0.095 ÷ (1 – 0.15) = 11.18%

36. A
Step 1: Total cost = 115 ft. × $36 per ft. = $4,140
Step 2: Portion paid by homeowner = $4,140 × (1 – 0.4) = $2,484
Step 3: Adjustment for lot across street = $2,484 ÷ 2 lots = $1,242 per lot

37. C
Step 1: Area of store = 50 ft. × 110 ft. = 5,500 sq. ft.
Step 2: Rent based on square footage = 5,500 sq. ft. × $32.50 per sq. ft. = $178,750
Step 3: Rent based on sales = ($625,000 – $150,000) × 0.0475 = $22,562.50
Step 4: Total rent = $178,750 + $22,562.50 = $201,312.50

38. C
Taxes owed from tax deduction = ($80,000 – $8,000) × 0.25 = $18,000

39. B
Taxes owed from tax credit = ($80,000 × 0.25) – $4,000 = $16,000

40. A
Step 1: Taxes owed from tax deduction = ($80,000 – $8,000) × 0.25 = $18,000
Step 2: Equivalent tax credit = ($80,000 × 0.25) – $18,000 = $2,000

CONCLUSION

All of my tools and training exercises about the real estate market are based on two principal factors that determine human nature: Emotion and logic.

The former is based on a non-rational evaluation of what we think, how we feel, and how we interact with the world around us. For example, certain types of music, art, fashion, and design evoke certain experiences within us that can't be explained by reason.

The latter is based on cold, hard facts. This is the part of human nature that doesn't factor in emotions, feelings, or the non-rational principles of reason. In the real estate profession, this includes tangible aspects like square footage, neighborhood profiles, and comparable sales history.

The blending of these two factors is what accounts for much of the information that you will encounter as a real estate agent. For the purposes of this book, we have focused on the rational, in an effort to help lay the foundation for you to cultivate your softer skills as you advance through your career. Once you feel that you've mastered the tools and principles presented in this book, I invite you to visit www.flaggship.com for additional training exercises and teaching aids to assist you on your path toward becoming a licensed agent.

ABOUT THE AUTHOR

Josh Flagg is one of America's most successful and sought-after luxury real estate agents, having completed more than two billion dollars in residential real estate sales in the past decade. He is currently recognized by *The Wall Street Journal* as one of the top-ranked agents in the nation by sales volume, and as a Top 25 Real Estate Agent by *The Hollywood Reporter*. Josh has been the agent for many of Hollywood's biggest names including Merv Griffin, Adam Levine, Steve Aoki, Shonda Rhymes, and Chicago's Robert Lamm, to name a few. He has also represented, for many years, distinguished families including the Debartolos, the Bloomingdales, the Gettys, and many more. In 2012, Josh earned the distinction of being named to Forbes' exclusive "30 Under 30" list.

Josh is world-renowned for his role in Bravo's hit television series *Million Dollar Listing: Los Angeles*. He has been on the series since its inception in 2006, and he also regularly appears as a real estate expert in various other media including CNBC's *Squawk Box*, NBC's *Today Show*, CBS's *The Insider*, Bravo's *Watch What Happens Live*, ABC's *Good Morning America*, as well as various Fox Business programs. He also regularly appears in the pages of *The Wall Street Journal*, *Los Angeles Times*, *Forbes Magazine*, and *Variety*, among others.

Today, Josh is expanding his influence in the real estate world by creating training programs, online courses, and other teaching platforms to help agents navigate the complex residential real estate market. Real estate sales have numerous challenges associated with them, and Josh's mission is to make it easier for agents to achieve success and experience as much passion and love for selling houses as he has.

INDEX

Made in the USA
San Bernardino, CA
10 July 2018